Today's Greatest Alternative Medicines

Contents

Report 1
Pain Free in Seconds

PAIN FREE IN SECONDS

Contents

Chapter 1

One-time charge for long-time relief from chronic pain

In the May 1998 issue of *Members Alert,* HSI wrote about the FDA ban on one of the products we had featured several years before—a pain relieving blanket made from a fabric called Farabloc™. That's right: It's not just vitamins, herbs, and other natural supplements the FDA wants to get rid of—it's all alternative therapies, even items as harmless as a blanket.

Although it demonstrated fantastic success for pain management and had proven itself in clinical studies, the FDA removed Farabloc from the American market. It declared that there was insufficient evidence to "adequately demonstrate the safety and effectiveness of Farabloc" technology.

In addition to the clinical trials supporting it, it had also earned enthusiastic endorsements from physicians, insurance agencies, and consumer groups. And the feedback we received from scores of HSI members related near-miraculous results—including the elimination of knee pain, stiff necks, stump pain, arthritis, hip pain, muscle sprains, menstrual cramps, and migraines. In fact, one of our own staff members swore that the Farabloc blanket was the best—and only—relief she ever found from constant lower back pain caused by a slipped disk.

But, again, sometimes when a product works—really works—and the market demands access to it, things have a way of re-emerging. And Farabloc happens to be one of those things that really, truly works.

A new way to weather your painful symptoms

For generations, anecdotal evidence has demonstrated that people can predict weather changes based on symptom flare-ups they feel in their bodies. Maybe you've noticed your own joints aching just before a rainstorm or when a cold front moves in. Well, in 1969, a German scientist named Frieder Kempe began researching those claims to determine if there was any hard evidence to back them up.

He theorized that the shifts in electromagnetic fields causing weather changes may also be behind the physical symptom changes people experience during these times. To test out his theory, he created his own version of something called a Faraday cage and used it on his father, a WWII veteran who had lost a limb in combat and suffered phantom limb pain during climate and other environmental changes.

A Faraday Cage is a physical shield that completely blocks external electrical fields from coming into contact with—or affecting in any way—the object beneath it.

Granted, it sounds rather difficult to employ in real-world applications, but it's actually used every day in nearly every hospital. MRI machines utilize the concept of the Faraday cage as a means to keep the room free from radiation. The actual "cage" used for MRIs is made of an iron-containing metal, arranged in a grid pattern, that blocks high level electromagnetic frequencies or radiation from escaping the tunnel.

The fabric Kempe developed for his Farabloc blanket is made in the same way, only with a much finer grid. Of course, Farabloc isn't protecting outside environments—it's actually doing the reverse: protecting you—and all your cells—from the impact of those electromagnetic fields that cause atmospheric and environmental fluctuations.

To create his first prototype, Kempe hired a Belgian-based firm to spin fine steel mesh onto nylon thread. He then hired a German firm to weave the fibers into cloth. The result was a thick, stiff, uncomfortable, itchy fabric. Not exactly ideal—but it worked. When his father tried it, he reported complete relief from his phantom limb pain.

So following his initial success, Kempe set out to create a thinner, softer, more comfortable fabric.

He tested cotton and linen versions, but found them both less durable than the nylon fabric he'd originally chosen. The final version available today, is made of microthin threads of stainless steel fibers woven with nylon. This lightweight fabric looks and feels like linen, and, with proper care, it can last for years.

Weaving the way to relief from phantom limb pain, muscle fatigue, and even fibromyalgia

Since our first report on Farabloc in July 1996, many studies have been done—perhaps as a vehement retort to the FDA's position that there was insufficient evidence to "adequately demonstrate the [product's] safety and effectiveness."

Most of the research has been devoted to phantom limb pain like the kind Kempe's father experienced. However, Farabloc is also holding its own in demonstrating relief for other conditions—from arthritis to fibromyalgia.

One award-winning double-blind, cross-over study published in January of 2000 examined the effects of Farabloc and a placebo fabric on a condition called delayed-onset muscle soreness (DOMS), which occurs following strenuous exercise.

The researchers concluded that Farabloc worked significantly better than the placebo at reducing post-exercise stiffness and soreness. It also reduced the subsequent build-up of lactic acid and free-radical damage.

And I recently got a sneak peak at two not-yet-published studies conducted by Gerhard L. Bach, M.D., professor of medicine/rheumatology at the University of Munich in Germany on the use of Farabloc to treat fibromyalgia. Although the studies were small, they concluded that Farabloc showed a strong positive effect on the pain and tenderness associated with this condition.

As I said, these studies are so recent they haven't even been published yet—so you're among the first people to hear about Farabloc's proven effects on fibromyalgia. There's so little available to help alleviate this debilitating condition that these studies, and the re-introduction of Farabloc to the U.S. market, may revolutionize the future of fibromyalgia therapy—and dramatically improve the lives of those people afflicted with it.

The faces peeking out from under this "miracle blanket"

When I spoke to Pat Winterton, president of ABC Health Solutions, Farabloc's U.S. distributor, I wasn't at all surprised when she told me she had a personal motive for bringing Farabloc back into the U.S.—her husband. After a stroke, he was left partially paralyzed and suffering from terrible nerve pain. Although she admits that Farabloc does not help everyone and that each person's response time varies—due to environment, lifestyle, disease, etc.—she will tell you that it's the only thing that has truly brought her husband any relief. And Mr. Winterton isn't the only one getting a long-sought-after reprieve from pain. Check out what some other people have experienced:

Three years ago, Pauletta L. was diagnosed with peripheral neuropathy. She says her feet would get ice cold, lose feeling, and generally make it very hard for her to walk comfortably. Her doctor told her that there was really no treatment for the condition, but he did prescribe her a drug that he said would relieve her symptoms somewhat.

But then, Pauletta explained, a friend gave her a Farabloc blanket to try.

"I slept with this blanket around my feet that night," Pauletta told me, "and as soon as I woke up in the morning and stepped on my floor, I could feel a difference in my feet...My feet still occasionally get cold, but I simply wrap them in the blanket for a few moments and they are OK again."

"To keep my feet feeling good I sleep with the blanket over them two or three nights per week. I am eternally grateful to my friend for this gift that she gave me. I can now walk around and shop for hours without needing to sit and put my feet up. They are no longer swollen after a long day on them as they used to be.

"I was a skeptic. Even my doctor asked me if I had to put an aluminum foil antenna on my head to get the blanket to work. I am a believer now. Drug free. Pain free. Swelling free. And, most importantly, no longer freezing cold. This product worked a miracle for me."

An investment in relief

Since its creation, Farabloc fabric has taken on many forms. There are, of course, the original blanket versions, which range in size from 12 inches by 30 inches to 34 inches by 58 inches. But there are also unique variations like socks, mitts, cummerbunds, and even full short- or long-sleeved jackets. You can also have an item custom-made, if you have a particular need that the other Farabloc products don't address.

Prices range from $50 all the way up to over $550, depending on which specific product and size you choose. So Farabloc isn't necessarily a bargain. But considering that it's reusable (and even machine washable, provided you don't wring it out), it may very well be an investment that you can continue to collect returns from for years to come.

And there are no side effects to worry about unless you happen to be allergic to nylon or steel.

To be quite honest, we're not sure what changed the FDA's mind about Farabloc. They've refused to see the light on numerous other highly effective natural products.

But regardless of the reason or motive behind the decision, it's great news for people who have been without this powerful pain reliever for the past six years. And, who knows? Maybe this will pave the way for the re-introduction of other previously banned products that could be a godsend for you or someone you love. See the Member Source Directory on page 14 for complete ordering information.

Chapter 2

Soothe your pain on contact

Arthritis...backache...sore muscles...aching joints...sprains...strains. As we get older, it seems as if pain becomes a constant companion. Just getting out of a chair can become challenging, let alone enjoying simple pleasures like gardening and strolling through the park. Taking aspirin helps, but it can eventually tear up your stomach. And prescription drugs have side effects that only compound the underlying problem. About 50 percent of the population is suffering from occasional aches and pains.[1]

Most medical schools don't teach pain relief

Mainstream medicine is finally becoming aware of the need to relieve pain. Hospitals now have pain-management teams. Palliative care—a relatively new medical specialty—was developed to address pain relief. Pain centers are also opening across the country as more and more people look for relief. But they all concentrate on mainstream "cures"— drugs and surgery, which are rife with uncomfortable and even life-threatening side effects.

Unfortunately, doctors aren't receiving much training in medical school about pain intervention. According to a survey of oncology surgeons, 90 percent of respondents said they received 10 hours or less of medical-school education on palliative care and 79 percent said they received no more than 10 hours of instruction in palliative care during their surgical residency.[2]

Healed injuries can continue to flare up over time

Effective pain management is a complex issue, because your body responds with all its defenses to protect and heal an injury. When you injure yourself, your body sends protective fluids, such as histamine, bradykinin, prostaglandin, and substance P, to surround and heal the area. But they can also irritate the injury over time.

Another problem associated with pain is referred to as the "snowball effect." This is the result of pain caused by injury and inflammation, which in turn causes distress and, as a result, continued pain and inflammation. This cyclic pattern snowballs and results in discomfort even after the original injury has been healed.

While you may have done everything possible to heal an injury for good, that doesn't mean the hurt will leave once your injury has healed. Most people can relate to occasional flare ups from past injuries, or subsequent pulled muscles or aching backs that come from trying to compensate for the original injury.

Putting a stop to the pain cycle

Finding a way to stop the pain cycle has been a goal of Health Sciences Institute panelist Jon Barron. Recently, he teamed up with Ron Manwarren of Royal Botanicals in the development of a unique topical pain reliever that is safe and completely free of the side effects of dangerous pharmaceutical pain killers. While Barron was refining an all-natural transport system that would send herbal extracts through the skin, Manwarren had just finished formulating a healing oil based on traditional herbs— but lacked a botanical-based foundation to transport it. When Manwarren brought his new formula to Barron, their combined efforts resulted in a formula available in a product called Soothanol X2.

While over-the-counter topical products commonly contain one, two, or three pain-relieving substances, such as methyl salicylate, menthol, and camphor, Soothanol X2 has 10 proven painkillers.

Because Soothanol X2 is an easyspreading and potent liquid, only a few drops are needed. Soothing pain relief is delivered on contact. In fact, we tested it informally here at the Health Sciences Institute Baltimore office.

The scented ingredients in Soothanol X2 are mild— contrary to the overpowering smells of most over-the-counter products. Although cayenne can deliver a warming or hot sensation, much of that sensation depends on the type of injury you're treating and your sensitivity to cayenne. Of the five people who tested our sample bottle here in the office, only one commented that he felt an uncomfortable amount of heat.

Because a little goes a long way, the cost per application is extremely economical. See the Member Source Directory for ordering information. Unfortunately, this product is not available in Australia.

Chapter 3

Want relief from migraine headaches?
A few drops under the tongue may be all you need

A new product called MigraSpray landed on my desk-and from the initial reports I'm getting, it sounds like it might be the answer to your prayers if you suffer from migraines.

A colleague of mine has been fighting migraines for nearly 30 years, and has tried everything from pills to injections to nasal sprays. She says her migraines are so intense, that she's willing to try almost anything. But unfortunately, nothing has given her much relief—until now.

Almost immediate relief—
and no side effects

So I gave her the sample I was sent. She tucked it away, and probably forgot about it. But the next time she developed a migraine, she remembered and dug it out. A couple of quick spritzes under the tongue, and almost immediately she could feel the pain dulling. Before taking MigraSpray, she had been sitting in a pitch dark room, because she couldn't stand even the light of a single bulb. After taking MigraSpray, she was able to turn on the lights—a simple thing that non-migraine sufferers like me take for granted.

She didn't experience any negative side effects, either-no "rebound" headache, no nasty taste, no stomach upset. She said she'll definitely use MigraSpray again, only next time, she'll use it sooner, before her headache fully blooms into a migraine.

Unique blend of four traditional
herbal medicines

So how does it work? It's a homeopathic blend of four traditional herbs: feverfew, goldenseal, dandelion, and polyporus officinalis. The lead ingredient, feverfew (tanacetum parthenium) is a traditional herbal remedy for migraines and clinical studies have supported its ability to prevent migraines and reduce their severity.[1,2] Research suggests that feverfew's active ingredients are phytochemicals called

sesquiterpene lactones, particularly one component known as parthenolide. Scientists believe parthenolide may relieve migraines by inhibiting cerebral blood vessel dilation. Parthenolide exerts anti-inflammatory properties by inhibiting platelet aggregation and prostaglandin synthesis, as well as the release of serotonin from platelets.[3]

The other ingredients in MigraSpray are not traditional headache remedies, but each contributes factors that may complement feverfew's anti-inflammatory power. Goldenseal (hydrastis rhizoma), which contains the amebicide phytochemical berberine, has traditionally been used to treat cholera. But herbal authorities also report that goldenseal can work as a sedative and an anti-inflammatory, particularly relieving inflammation in the mucous membranes of the head and throat.[4] Dandelion (Taraxacum denleonis) is best known as a potent diuretic and laxative, and is a rich source of potassium. And P. officinalis, a fungus commonly known as white agaric or larch agaric, is known in herbal medicine to have effects on the sympathetic and spinal nervous systems, and is used as a remedy for spasmodic nerve pain and epilepsy.[6]

In a private study conducted by MigraSpray's manufacturer, 41 migraine sufferers were divided into two groups to test the effectiveness of MigraSpray against a placebo. Nearly 88 percent of the MigraSpray group saw some level of improvement from using the spray, while about 66 percent of them reported full to complete improvement. Even better, the average elapsed time between administration and relief in the MigraSpray group was just six and a half minutes.[7]

MigraSpray is safe for most people, but the product label does warn pregnant and lactating women not to use it. My research also indicates that feverfew can alter clotting time.[8] Therefore if you are taking warfarin or other blood thinners, consult your physician and get your clotting times checked. Your medical dose may need to be lowered or feverfew may be contraindicated. Also, one study indicates that non-steroidal anti-inflammatory drugs, or NSAIDS, can negate feverfew's efficacy in fighting migraines, so you may want to avoid taking NSAIDS together with MigraSpray (also probably a good idea in light of the blood-thinning consideration).[9]

MigraSpray is available at many drug retailers, via the Internet, or by phone (see the Member Source Directory on page 14 for complete ordering information). It's hard to say how long one bottle might last, as it depends on the frequency of use. The product label recommends administering 10 sprays under the tongue at the first signs of an impending headache. After administration, wait at least 30 seconds before swallowing. If you don't feel relief after five minutes, you can repeat the process one more time.

Chapter 4

Tibetan medicine relieves chronic leg pain

There are few things worse than losing your freedom to walk—not being able to go where you want to go or do what you want to do. But it's what thousands face each day, due to the often excruciating pain of intermittent claudication, a condition in which a decrease in blood to the legs brings about a reduction in oxygen to your lower extremities (which triggers the pain). The more you walk, the more oxygen is needed by your legs, hence, the greater the discomfort. This disorder can lead, if left untreated, to gangrene, and is linked to other serious health problems, such as hardening of the arteries and heart disease.

Mainstream medicine has little to offer. You can try a medication like Pentoxifylline, with undesirable side effects (including extreme dizziness and vomiting) and questionable effectiveness.[1] Or, as is often the case with Western medicine, you can opt for the ordeal of surgery.

An effective solution without side effects

But thankfully, you don't have to settle for the limited choices of the West. Eastern medicine has a better option—one that's both effective and free of side effects. Padma Basic is an herbal mixture from Tibet that's quickly proving to be a powerful treatment for intermittent claudication. Formulated over 2,000 years ago, the preparation is a complex combination of 19 different herbs that combine to produce a powerful antioxidant.

While the mixture was originally intended to treat illnesses brought on by the overconsumption of meat, fat, and alcohol, its broader uses are now being discovered.

In a dramatic double-blind placebo study held in 1985, intermittent claudication patients on Padma were found to have a 100 percent increase in the distance they could walk pain free. In addition, the drug was well tolerated by the patients.[2] Since then, a series of studies have confirmed these original results.[3-6]

Not surprisingly, the phenomenon of Padma has spread from the mountains of Tibet through Israel, Switzerland, England, and the rest of Europe. Now, Padma Basic is available to HSI members through the Econugenics. They've set up a U.S. order bank, to make it easier for our American members to obtain this fantastic product.

The recommended dosage for Padma Basic is two tablets taken three times a day for the first four weeks. After that, take two tablets daily. Please be aware that it could take a minimum of three months for you to receive the full benefit of this treatment. Refer to the back of this report for ordering information.

Chapter 5

Replace Vioxx with the 2 latest all-natural arthritis remedies

At HSI, we've covered natural arthritis remedies many times over the years. And now that Vioxx, the pharmaceutical drug many people relied on for pain relief, has been pulled from the market, we thought it was the perfect time to report on two of the latest all-natural, safe remedies we've come across-Kaprex and SierraSil.

A new day in arthritis treatment

In case you're not familiar with the Vioxx situation, here's a recap: Vioxx's manufacturer, Merck, recently launched a large, randomized trial of 2,600 patients with colon polyps in hopes of proving that Vioxx could help their condition. In the process, though, Merck discovered that 3.5 percent of the patients taking Vioxx suffered heart attacks or strokes vs. 1.9 percent taking a placebo. Based on this finding, Merck withdrew the drug from the market altogether.

This must have come as a devastating blow to those people who depended on Vioxx for arthritis relief.

But the good news is you're not limited anymore to treatments like Vioxx that just mask pain or put you at risk for unrelated, more serious problems. The natural joint relief products we're focusing on today don't trick your body by blocking pain receptors-they actually stop the cause of the damage to the joint.

Block your body's damage-causing signals

First, Kaprex. It works by interfering with signals in the body that result in the production of damaging compounds that cause your pain and negatively impact cartilage and other joint tissues.

To find the best candidates for the formula, product developers at Metagenics' MetaProteomics™ Research Center screened over 150 natural substances. These in-vitro tests examined each potential ingredient for efficacy by studying its effect on cell protein synthesis and activity.

The researchers compiled and analyzed thousands of data points and selected three based on their outstanding effectiveness—oleanolic acid, rosemary, and hops.

Recent data suggests that components of hops-such as reduced isoalpha acids-may inhibit the formation of inflammation-causing prostaglandins.[1]

The form added to Kaprex is a proprietary extract of hops called Luduxin™.

Oleanolic acid is derived from olive leaf extract. Research indicates that it may support joint health as a pain reliever as well as protect against potential damage to your stomach lining.

And rosemary leaf extract stimulates circulation and eases pain by increasing blood supply.

Although these herbs were chosen for their individual arthritis-relieving properties, the product developers found that when they put all of them together the effects were even better. Think of it as herbal teamwork.

According to Dr. Joseph Debe, a chiropractor and board-certified nutritionist, one of the things that sets Kaprex apart from other arthritis remedies, including over-the-counter pain relievers, is that it doesn't appear to cause stomach damage or irritation. Researchers have found that Kaprex has "minimal GI cell activity and therefore a high level of predicted GI safety."

Both non-steroidal anti-inflammatory drugs and Kaprex work by reducing the concentration of a body chemical called prostaglandin E2 (PGE2), but they do so through different mechanisms. PGE2 is a powerful hormone-like chemical that is responsible for producing the majority of the pain and inflammation associated with arthritis and other conditions.

Another impact of accumulated PGE2 is heightened sensitivity in your nerve fibers where even the slightest movement can cause inordinate pain. It takes a while for it to build up, so at first you may just be a little stiff and sore. But the symptoms increase progressively until any joint movement becomes a challenge and pain an unwanted constant companion.

The non-steroidal anti-inflammatory drugs reduce levels of PGE2 by inhibiting the activity of the enzymes that manufacture it. But, unfortunately, not only is PGE2 production reduced in joints, it's also reduced in gastrointestinal tissues. And a certain level of PGE2 is necessary to keep gastrointestinal tissues healthy. When PGE2 is deficient, it can contribute to ulcer formation.

On the other hand, Kaprex works through a safer, "upstream" mechanism. It reduces the excessive formation of the PGE2- producing enzymes, rather than inhibiting their activity. It appears to actually reduce the message sent to the genes to manufacture the enzyme. This makes all the difference in production of gastrointestinal injury. The net effect is that Kaprex is active in joint tissues without affecting the gastrointestinal tract.

A recent study examined Kaprex's absorbability and bioavailability. Six subjects supplemented on different days with either one Kaprex tablet, three Kaprex tablets, or one Celebrex capsule. Their blood was drawn prior to dosing and at one, two, four, six, and eight hours after dosing. The blood samples were analyzed for their ability to reduce PGE2 levels.

Kaprex worked quickly and maintained effectiveness for hours, with activity beginning to decrease at eight hours. One tablet of Kaprex appeared to be as effective as one capsule of Celebrex and worked more rapidly. As you might expect, three tablets of Kaprex produced a significantly greater effect than just one tablet.[2]

Kaprex is available in 30- and 90-tablet bottles. The recommended dose is one tablet three times daily. According to Metagenics, you'll know whether it works for you within seven to 10 days. If it doesn't help, you can send back the bottle for a full refund.

The volcano cure for joint breakdown

The other product is called SierraSil, and it's made from a distinct, naturally occurring volcanic mineral deposit mined only in an exclusive location high in the Sierra Mountains.

This distinct volcanic compound, which contains a uniquely balanced blend of 65 macro and trace minerals, has been shown to support joint mobility and flexibility, and based on what I've been told, is changing people's lives.

Even the manufacturing process is unique. It occurs naturally in a unique textured rock form, which is extracted from one specific surface mine site located five hours from the closest city. Once it's taken from the ground, it's put in barrels and moved to the manufacturer's location where it is pulverized, heated to ensure that there are no micro-organisms present in the formula, then put into capsules.

Decrease cartilage breakdown by up to 73 percent in just one week

The idea of volcanic rock used as a supplement to relieve arthritis pain struck us as odd, to say the least. So we checked in with our medical adviser, Dr. Martin Milner, to see what he could tell us. According to Dr. Milner, minerals derived from rock rather than plants are relatively difficult to absorb (usually 10 percent at best). He also cautioned that the distribution of elements in the volcanic rock may or may not be in safe concentrations and ratios. We went back to Sierra Mountain Minerals for an additional explanation regarding these concerns. They told us that "quite the opposite is true with the SierraSil minerals, 45% are present naturally in a highly absorbable form, while the rest are present in a mineral rich clay compound that is not absorbed but passes right through the body detoxifying as it collects toxins and heavy metals on its way out."

An in vitro study using human cartilage tissues and cells from osteoarthritis (OA) patients found that SierraSil reduced the breakdown of cartilage cells by 68 to 73 percent in just one week. According to the lead researcher of the study, Mark Miller, Ph.D., "SierraSil... may offer exciting new approaches to limiting the joint destruction and lack of mobility associated with arthritis."[3]

Based on the results of this pilot study, the mineral complex was investigated in a randomized, double-blind, placebo-controlled human clinical trial involving 120 patients with OA of the knee. The study findings showed significant reduction in pain, stiffness, inflammation and improvements in joint functionality within one month of therapy. Dramatic improvements were evident within one to two weeks.

Testimonials have been flooding in. They relate some pretty powerful stories. One woman's letter said, "I cried when I noticed for the first time in years I wasn't thinking about my pain." Another person commented, "After getting partial relief from natural remedies for joint problems I have finally found complete relief."

SierraSil comes in either capsule or powder form. They're both available in many health food stores across the country, and we've offered a phone-order source in the Member Source Directory on page 14. The recommended dosage for SierraSil is three capsules once daily on an empty stomach or one scoop of powder daily, mixed into juice, water, or food.

Chapter 6

Raw bar favorite offers arthritis relief

Imagine if you didn't need pain relievers every-day? Our research has uncovered something totally new—a completely safe and natural food extract that may be the most powerful anti-inflammatory compound ever discovered.

It's called Lyprinol, an active lipid fraction isolated from the New Zealand green-lipped mussel, or Perna canaliculus. According to centuries-old tradition, native Maoris believe that eating the green-lipped mussel leads to a long and healthy life. And, in fact, medical statistics show that arthritis and rheumatic disorders are unknown among the coastal-dwelling Maori.

Scientists have now determined that the anti-arthritic properties of the green-lipped mussel are due to the unique configuration of certain polyun-saturated fatty acids (or PUFAs) called Eicosate-traenoic Acids (ETAs). Related to the Omega-3 fatty acids found in fish, flaxseed, and perilla oil, ETAs display more intense and targeted anti-inflammatory and anti-arthritic activity than any other known PUFA or Omega-3 fatty acid.

Research in the 1970s and 1980s confirmed that something in the New Zealand green-lipped mussel had the ability to erase arthritic pain and stiffness. A double-blind, placebo-controlled trial conducted in 1980 at the Victoria Hospital in Glasgow, Eng-land, tested a powdered mussel supplement on 66 arthritis patients.[1] At the start of the six-month trial, all of the subjects had failed to respond to conventional treatment and were scheduled for surgery to repair badly damaged joints.

At the close of the trial, the researchers reported improvements in 68 percent of the rheumatoid arthritis (RA) patients and in 39 percent of the osteoarthritis (OA) patients. The scientists also noted the low incidence of adverse side effects.

Nearly two decades later scientists perfect the solution

For the next 18 years, leading scientists from uni-versities and research labs in Australia, Japan, and France worked together to understand the secret locked within the green-lipped mussel. Step by incremental step, the scientists managed to identify the active biological fraction of the green-lipped mussel, isolate it without destroying its essential properties, cleanse it of impurities, stabilize it, and standardize its potency for reliable results.

At every step of the way, clinical and laboratory studies confirmed that scientists were moving in the right direction. Their excitement mounted as each phase yielded a more potent and powerful com-pound. Even early versions of the green-lipped mus-sel extracts were found to be more effective than aspirin and ibuprofen in reducing inflammation.

But inflammation isn't the only thing it helped. In 1986, a trial of 53 RA patients, conducted by the Societé Française de Biologic et Dietique (SFBD) in Dijon, France, found that the green-lipped mussel extract reduced pain by 62 percent after six months, while those on a placebo had a 20 percent increase in pain.[2]

Lyprinol: 200 times more effective than high potency fish oil in controlling swelling

Ultimately, scientists zeroed in on the ETAs in the green-lipped mussel as the active ingredients responsible for its remarkable anti-arthritic effects. This specific grouping of ETAs is not found in any other known substance. The methods used to con-centrate these active components in a pure and sta-ble form have been granted patents in several coun-tries. The final result is now available as Lyprinol.

Researchers at the University of Queensland in Brisbane, Australia, studied the efficacy of Lyprinol using laboratory animals with adjuvant-induced polyarthritis, which is the closest model for rheuma-toid arthritis in humans.[3]

When administered as an oral supplement, Lypri-nol reduced arthritis-related swelling in the animal's paws by more than 90 percent. It was also effective when rubbed directly into the affected area.

Comparisons of Lyprinol to other natural lipids, or fatty acids, known to be helpful in treat-ing arthritis and inflammation, tested Lyprinol against flax oil, evening primrose oil, Norwegian salmon oil, and MaxEPA (a high potency fish oil product). Of these, Lyprinol was the most effec-tive in preventing arthritis-related swelling, reduc-ing swelling by 79 percent. MaxEPA was the next best at 50 percent. However, the real story is the dosages used to achieve these results.

Achieving a 50 percent effectiveness rate required a dosage of 2000 mg/kg body weight of MaxEPA. But the effective dosage of Lyprinol was only 20 mg/kg—or 1/100 the amount. Extrapolations from these results suggest that the anti-inflammatory compounds in Lyprinol are 200 times more potent than MaxEPA (and 350 times more potent than evening primrose oil).

Outperforms arthritis drugs without harmful side effects

Researchers also compared the effectiveness of Lyprinol to that of the prescription arthritis drug indomethacin, the mainstream drug of choice at the time of the study. A dosage of 5 mg/kg of Lyprinol was 97 percent effective in reducing swelling, while indomethacin was only 83 percent effective at the same dosage. Unlike indomethacin, Lyprinol is non-toxic and essentially free of side effects. In a 2000 study, researchers found that when compared to NSAIDs, three Lyprinol was "non-gastro toxic."[4]

Recommendations for use

Lyprinol is recommended for the alleviation of inflammatory conditions, including osteoarthritis, rheumatoid arthritis, and virally-induced arthritis.

While Lyprinol appears to be the most powerful anti-inflammatory and arthritis pain reliever yet discovered, it still won't rebuild or restore previously damaged cartilage. For the most complete healing of arthritis, we recommend you combine Lyprinol with a natural joint building supplement containing glucosamine and chondroitin.

Recommended amounts: The amount needed for optimal results can vary widely for each individual, but range between two and four capsules per day. A higher amount (up to six capsules per day) can be used for the first one to two weeks of use. It can take up to four weeks to evaluate the full benefit. In addition, the research suggests that rubbing Lyprinol onto swollen and tender joints can help relieve pain and swelling. To do this, simply open the capsule and squeeze the contents onto the affected area. See the Member Source Directory in the back of this report to learn how you can order Lyprinol.

Chapter 7

Relieve back pain with this inexpensive natural remedy

When you have back pain, it affects everything you do. Everyday activities like carrying groceries or walking around the block can become a major challenge.

The mainstream offers NSAIDs, which can be effective for short-term relief - but can also cause negative side effects like gastrointestinal damage. The new prescription NSAIDs called COX-2 inhibitors are designed to avoid those problems— but they can be quite expensive. For many people, neither provides a good option.

But there is an all-natural remedy that is being shown to alleviate lower back pain as effectively as prescription drugs, without the risk of side effects —and without the steep price tag.

It's called willow bark extract, and it's been used by herbalists for many years to treat many types of pain. Several clinical trials have supported willow bark's efficacy against back pain. Now a new study shows that willow bark extract is just as effective as a popular prescription drug—at significantly less expense.

Willow bark proven as effective as Vioxx— without the health risks

Before Merk withdrew Vioxx from the market a German study tested the effectiveness of willow bark extract against rofecoxib, the generic form of Vioxx. The researchers recruited 228 people between the ages of 18 and 80. All had experienced lower back pain for at least six months, and their pain couldn't be attributed to any identifiable cause, like arthritis, disc prolapse, or trauma. Before treatment began, the participants rated their pain on several commonly used indices.

For four weeks, half the group took four capsules of willow bark extract each day, while another half took a single 12.5 mg tablet of rofecoxib daily. The two groups were similar in age, sex, height, weight, and duration and severity of pain. During the study period, the participants were contacted by phone each week, and then the assessments were completed again at the end of the four weeks.

Here's what they found: willow bark extract was just as effective as rofecoxib at alleviating lower back pain. Both produced similar reductions on the various measurement tools used to assess the participant's pain. And while neither therapy caused many side effects in this study, the researchers noted that the side effects from rofecoxib "tended to be more severe" and "caused more withdrawals from the study." The most common side effect from both therapies was "gastrointestinal complaints," and four people had allergic reactions to the willow bark extract.

No reason to accept ANY side effect risks

The active ingredient in willow bark extract is salicin, a natural anti-inflammatory. In the study, the extract was standardized to contain 15 percent salicin, and the participants took a dose equal to 240 mg of salicin each day.

With the availability of a safe, natural option like willow bark extract, there's no reason to take those risks. Based on the study results, you should watch closely to see that no allergic reaction occurs. But assuming it doesn't, this may just be the relief you've been looking for to help ease your lower back pain—and it won't break the bank, either.

Member Source Directory

Farabloc, ABC Health Solutions; ph. (253)631-8270 or (206)949-2097; fax (253)639-2467; www.abchealthsolutions.biz.

Soothanol X2 NorthStar Nutritionals; P.O. Box 970 Frederick, MD 21705. (888)856-1489, www.northstarnutritionals.com.

MigraSpray, Nature Well, Inc., 110 West C Street, Suite 1300, San Diego, CA 92101; tel: (800)454-6790; www.migraspray.com. 1 bottle costs US$39.95 plus US$7.95 for shipping.

Padma Basic Econugenics; tel: (707)521-3370; www.econugenics.com. A 180-tablet bottle is US$94.95 plus shipping and handling.

Kaprex, Center for Natural Medicine Dispensary; tel. (888)305-4288 or (503)232-0475; www.cnm-inc.com. A 90-tablet bottle costs US$39.96 plus shipping.

SierraSil, Sierra Mountain Minerals, Inc.; tel. (877)743-7720; www.sierrasil.com. 45 capsules US$19.95; 90 capsules US$34.95.

Lyprinol The Vitamin Shoppe; 2101 91st Street, North Bergen, NJ 07047; tel: (866)293-3367; www.vitaminshoppe.com.

Please note: HSI receives no compensation for providing editorial coverage for the products that appear in this report. HSI is a subsidiary of the same holding company as NDI Solutions, the distributor of NorthStar Nutritionals, RealAdvantage and Pure Country Naturals supplements.

HSI verifies all product information when reports are written; however, pricing and availability can change by the time reports are delivered. We regret that not all products are available in all locations worldwide.

The above statements have not been evaluated by the U.S. Food and Drug Administration. These products are not intended to diagnose, treat, cure, or prevent any disease.

References

Soothe your pain on contact
1 *Lancet* 2000;355(9199): 233-34
2 Reuters Health Information, April 23, 2000

Want relief from migraine headaches? A few drops under the tongue may be all you need...
1 Murphy JJ, Heptistall S, Mitchell JR "Randomized double-blind placebo-controlled trial of feverfew in migraine preparations" *Lancet* 1988 Jul;2(8604):189-192
2 Johnson ES, Kadam NP, et al "Efficacy of feverfew as prophylactic treatment of migraine" *Br Med J* (Clin Res Ed) 1985 Aug;291(6495):569-573
3 www.migraspray.com
4 Hoffman D Herbal Materia Medica http://www.healthy.net
5 ibid
6 Felter HW, Lloyd JU King's American Dispensatory http://www.ibilio.org/herbmed
7 Blum JM, Marshall P, "Herbal someopathic support for the treatment of migraine-type headache symptoms" Executive Summary, NatureWell Inc. LaJolla CA Aug 29, 2001
8 Miller LG "Herbal medicinals: selected clinical considerations" *Arch Intern Med* 1998 Nov;158(20):2200-2211
9 ibid

Tibetan medicine relieves chronic leg pain
1 MCP Hahnemann University Libraries, Health Reviews on the Internet, "A Meta-analysis of the Treatment of Intermittent Claudication," Richard Neil, M.D.
2 Schweizerische Medizinische Wochenschrift 1985;115(22): 752-56
3 *Angiology* 1998;44(11): 863-67
4 *Journal of Vascular Investigation* 1998;4: 129-36
5 *The Express*, March 31, 1999
6 *Annales Academiae Medicae Stetinensis* 1991;37: 191-202

Replace Vioxx with the 2 latest all-natural arthritis remedies
1 Babish JG, Howell T. Proprietary Research Report. San Clemente, CA: MetaProteomics, Inc. 2003. and Yamamoto K, Wang J, Yamamoto S, et al. Suppression of cyclooxygenase-2 gene transcription by humulon of beer hop extract studied with reference to glucocorticoid. FEBS Lett 2000;465:103-06.
2 http://www.newliving.com/issues/oct_2003/articles/newnatural.html
3 Miller MJ et al. "Suppression of human cartilage degradation and chondrocyte activation by a unique mineral supplement (SierraSil™) and a Cat's Claw Extract, Vincaria®." JANA. 7, 2:1-8, 2004.

Raw bar favorite offers arthritis relief
1 *Practioner* 1980; 224: 955-60
2 *Gazette Medicale* 1986; 93(38): 111-16
3 *Inflammopharmacology* 1997;5 : 237-46
4 *Allergie et Immunologie* 2000; 32(7): 272-78

Relieve back pain with this inexpensive natural remedy
1 *Rheumatology* 2001; 40:1388-1393

Report 2
Cancer's Kryptonite:
Amazing New Cancer Killers

CANCER'S KRYPTONITE: AMAZING NEW CANCER KILLERS

Contents

Chapter 1

Cancer's kryptonite: HSI panelist tests breakthrough seaweed cancer treatment

It's a weed and a slimy weed at that. But unlike the ones that invade your lawn, this weed might actually do you some good. It has been credited as a primary cause for record-low cancer rates in Okinawa, Japan. It was used—with reported success—to treat and prevent radiation sickness following the Chernobyl meltdown in Russia. It has yet to be tested in a single human clinical trial. But according to panelist Kohhei Makise, M.D., the Japanese medical community is being inundated with reports of how this medicinal seaweed has helped thousands of patients fight cancer.

Dr. Makise recently wrote us a long, excited e-mail discussing several new natural remedies that are producing impressive results among Japanese patients. But in this report, we decided to focus on a natural immune builder and cancer fighter that's so new to North America that we'd never heard of it before.

It's called fucoidan, and it's a complex of polysaccharides (carbohydrates) found in brown seaweed, most commonly in an Asia-Pacific variety known as *kombu* or *Laminaria japonica*. The seaweed has been a dietary staple in Japan since the second century B.C. And in Okinawa—which posts Japan's highest per capita rates of *kombu* consumption—it has reportedly produced considerable health benefits. Okinawa residents who eat an average of 1 gram of *kombu* (containing roughly 5 mg of fucoidan) daily enjoy some of the longest lifespans in Japan and the single lowest cancer rate in the country.

Seaweed extract causes cancer cells to self-destruct

In the 1990s, scientists identified fucoidan as the primary immune-building substance in brown seaweed and began to test it.

In one case, researchers injected female lab rats with a carcinogen known to induce mammary tumors. They fed half of the rats a standard diet, fed the other half a standard diet plus daily helpings of brown seaweed containing fucoidan, and monitored the animals for 26 weeks. The fucoidan appeared to convey two substantial benefits. First, the fucoidan fed rats developed fewer tumors than the control rats: 63 percent developed breast cancer vs. 76 percent of control rats. Second, the fucoidan-fed rats resisted developing tumors for longer periods of time: control rats typically developed tumors within 11 weeks, whereas fucoidan-fed rats remained cancer-free for 19 weeks.[1]

In other studies, oral and intravenous doses of brown seaweed proved anywhere from 61.9 to 95.2 percent effective in preventing the development of cancer in rats implanted with sarcoma cells.[2] One group of researchers described fucoidan as a "very potent antitumor agent in cancer therapy" after it inhibited the growth and spread of lung cancer in rats.[3] (That type of cancer is particularly resistant to chemotherapy.)

Various studies further demonstrated that fucoidan combats cancer in multiple ways:

- It causes certain types of rapidly growing cancer cells (including stomach cancer, colon cancer, and leukemia) to self-destruct (a process call apoptosis).
- It physically interferes with cancer cells' ability to adhere to tissue. That interference prevents the cancer from spreading (or metastasizing) to new areas.
- It enhances production of several immune mechanisms, including macrophages (white blood cells that destroy tumor cells), gamma interferon (proteins that activate macrophages and natural killer cells), and interleukin (compounds that help regulate the immune system).

Proof from the panelist's practice

But as Dr. Makise points out, fucoidan still needs to prove itself in large, double-blind, clinical trials involving creatures more evolved than guinea pigs.

Dr. Makise believes, however, that there is compelling evidence that fucoidan can help prevent cancer. Through his practice in Japan, Dr. Makise has seen that fucoidan can even help patients who already have cancer. He says that cancer patients benefit most by taking a combination of:

- fucoidan
- AHCC or other immune-enhancing mushrooms
- antioxidants, especially large doses of selenium
- Enterococcus feacalis—1 to 3 trillion dead bacterium (Enterococcus faecalis is a beneficial

bacterial found in the intestine. In addition to promoting healthy digestion and controlling bile acids that can cause colon cancer, it delivers certain immune-enhancing vitamins —like biotin and certain B vitamins—to the blood stream)

- essential daily vitamins and minerals (Dr. Makise recommends his patients take triple the recommended daily dosage of essential vitamins and minerals. He says it's especially important that cancer patients take daily supplements of selenium and zinc)
- a healthy lifestyle and diet that avoids meat, milk, and other animal proteins and fats.

"It is very effective for cancers that already exist, even end-stage metastases," Dr. Makise told us. "Each substance of this combination has a different mechanism to fight against cancer, so we get synergistic effects."

Fucoidan can be found in a product called Modipilan, manufactured by Fucoidan Sales. The product contains fucoidan, along with organic iodine—shown to promote maturation of the nervous system and alignate—a natural absorbent of radioactive elements, heavy metal, and free radicals. See the Member Source Directory at the back of this report for ordering information.

Chapter 2

News of astounding natural cancer killer nearly squashed forever

Recently, Health Sciences Institute uncovered a remarkable story about a natural cancer killer that had been kept under lock and key for over 20 years. With this information, the future of cancer treatment and the chances of survival look more promising than ever. There's a healing tree that grows deep within the Amazon rainforest in South America that could literally change how you, your doctor, and possibly the rest of the world think about curing cancer.

Since the 1970s, the bark, leaves, roots, fruit, and fruit seeds of the Amazonian Graviola tree have been studied in numerous laboratory tests and have shown remarkable results with this deadly disease.

Several years ago, a major pharmaceutical company began extensive independent research on it. They learned that certain extracts of the tree actually seek out, attack, and destroy cancer cells. Because the natural extracts themselves could not be patented, the company labored to create a synthetic copy that showed the same promise. After more than seven years of work behind closed doors, researchers at this company realized they couldn't duplicate the tree's natural properties with a patentable substance. So they shut down the entire project. It basically came down to this—if they couldn't make huge profits, they would keep the news of this possible cure a well-guarded secret. But one researcher couldn't bear that, and decided to risk his job with the hope of saving lives.

Seven years of silence broken

This conscience-driven researcher contacted Raintree Nutrition, a natural products company dedicated to harvesting plants from the Amazon. In the course of working with Raintree on another story, they shared the exciting Graviola breakthrough with us. Since then, we've been looking closely into the research to date on Graviola. One of the first scientific references to it in the United States was by the National Cancer Institute (NCI). In 1976, the NCI showed that the leaves and stems of this tree were effective in attacking and destroying malignant cells. But these results were part of an internal NCI report and were, for some reason, never made public.[1]

Since 1976, there have been several promising cancer studies on Graviola. However, the tree's extracts have yet to be tested on cancer patients. No double-blind clinical trials exist, and clinical trials are typically the benchmark mainstream doctors and journals use to judge a treatment's value. Nevertheless, our research has uncovered that Graviola has been shown to kill cancer cells in at least 20 laboratory tests.

The most recent study, conducted at Catholic University of South Korea, revealed that two chemicals extracted from Graviola seeds showed comparable results to the chemotherapy drug Adriamycin when applied to malignant breast and colon cells in test tubes.[2]

Another study, published in the *Journal of Natural Products*, showed that Graviola is not only comparable to Adriamycin—but dramatically outperforms it in laboratory tests. Results showed that it selectively killed colon cancer cells at "10,000 times the potency of Adriamycin."[3]

Perhaps the most significant result of the studies we've researched is that Graviola selectively seeks out and kills cancer cells—leaving all healthy, normal cells untouched. Chemotherapy indiscriminately seeks and destroys all actively reproducing cells, even normal hair and stomach cells, causing such devastating side effects as hair loss and severe nausea.

Grown and harvested by indigenous people in Brazil, Graviola is available in limited supply in the United States and is distributed through Raintree Nutrition. But now, you can be among the select few in the entire country to benefit from this pow-

erful treatment. We encourage you to consult with your doctor before beginning any new therapy, especially when treating cancer.

Graviola has been combined with seven other immune-boosting herbs in a product called N-Tense. As a dietary supplement, you should take six to eight capsules of N-Tense per day. Graviola and N-Tense are completely natural substances with no side effects apart from possible mild stomach upset at high dosages (in excess of 5 grams) if taken on an empty stomach.

If you've been diagnosed with cancer, you and your doctor should look into all the available treatment options. Graviola could just make all the difference in beating cancer. See the Member Source Directory at the back of this report for ordering information.

Chapter 3

Hybridized mushroom extract destroys cancer cells and provides powerful immune protection

Until now, the only way to get access to this remarkable immune booster was to live in Japan. For the last five years in Japan, people with cancer, AIDS, and other life-threatening illnesses—as well as healthy people who want to stay that way—have been revving up their immune systems, destroying tumor cells, and preventing cancer and other illnesses with a powerful extract called AHCC (activated hexose correlate compound). Now, AHCC is available to consumers in the United States.

AHCC is an extract of a unique hybridization of several kinds of medicinal mushrooms known for their immune-enhancing abilities. On their own, each mushroom has a long medical history in Japan, where their extracts are widely prescribed by physicians. But when combined into a single hybrid mushroom, the resulting active ingredient is so potent that dozens of rigorous scientific studies have now established AHCC to be one of the world's most powerful—and safe—immune stimulators.

In vitro animal and human studies confirm that AHCC effectively works against and, in some cases, even prevents the recurrence of liver cancer, prostate cancer, ovarian cancer, multiple myeloma, breast cancer, AIDS, and other life-threatening conditions, with no dangerous side effects.[1] In smaller doses, AHCC can also boost the immune function of

healthy people, helping to prevent infections and promote well-being.

Calling up your first line of defense

Our immune systems stand between us and the rest of the world. Without it, our bodies would be overrun by bacteria, viruses, parasites, fungi, and other invaders, infections would rapidly spread, and cancer cells would proliferate. Like a highly responsive and well-coordinated army, our immune systems are composed of a variety of specialized immune cells that identify, seek out, and destroy microbes, pathogens, and tumor cells.

First on the scene of possible trouble are the phagocytes and natural killer (NK) cells, which respond quickly to potential threats. Often referred to as the body's "front-line defense," these cells are constantly on the look out for any suspicious substances. NK cells latch onto the surface of substances or the outer membranes of cancer cells and inject a chemical hand grenade (called a granule) into the interior. Once inside, the granules explode and destroy the bacteria or cancer cell within five minutes. Itself undamaged, the NK cell then moves onto its next victim. In its prime, a NK cell can take on two cancer cells at the same time, speeding up the process.

Recent research shows that as we age, our immune systems function less efficiently. In particular, the ability of our NK cells to respond quickly and effectively declines with age and illness. When NK cells lose their ability to recognize or destroy invaders, health can deteriorate rapidly. Moderately low to dangerously low NK cell activity levels have been found in people with AIDS, cancer, immune deficiency, liver disorders, various infections, and other diseases. Because measurements of NK cell activity are closely correlated with one's chances of survival, anything that helps increase NK cell activity may help people treat, recover from, and/or prevent these illnesses.

Research finds remarkable immune system boost in multiple ways

Scientific studies of the extract AHCC, published in respected peer-reviewed journals such as *International Journal of Immunology*, *Anti-Cancer Drugs*, and *Society of Natural Immunity*, have established the health benefits and safety of AHCC more conclusively than nearly any other natural supplement.[2-4] What is especially remarkable about AHCC is that it consistently and effectively boosts immune system function. Specifically, AHCC:

- Stimulates cytokine (IL-2, IL-12, TNF, and INF) production, which stimulates immune function.
- Increases NK cell activity against diseased cells as much as 300 percent.
- Increases the formation of explosive granules within NK cells. The more ammunition each NK cell carries, the more invaders it can destroy.
- Increases the number and the activity of lymphocytes, specifically increasing T-cells up to 200 percent.
- Increases Interferon levels, which inhibits the replication of viruses and stimulates NK cell activity.

- Increases the formation of TNF, a group of proteins that help destroy cancer cells.

These dramatic immune effects translate into profound health benefits. A 1995 clinical trial reported in the *International Journal of Immunotherapy* showed that 3 grams of AHCC per day significantly lowered the level of tumor markers found in patients with prostate cancer, ovarian cancer, multiple myeloma, and breast cancer. This study documented complete remissions in six of 11 patients and significant increases in NK cell activity in nine of 11 patients. T- and B-cell activity levels also rose considerably.[5]

AHCC now available in the United States

After years of successful use in Japan, AHCC is available in the United States as the active ingredient in a product called ImmPower. Distributed by American BioSciences, ImmPower comes in gelatin capsules containing 500mg of AHCC (proprietary blend).

ImmPower can be taken in preventive or therapeutic doses and should be discussed with your personal physician. For prevention, the recommended dose is 1 gram per day taken as one 500mg capsule in the morning and again at night. This dose will help increase NK cell activity and support immune system functioning for good health and general well-being. For those with cancer, AIDS, or other life-threatening conditions, the research indicates a therapeutic dose of two capsules in the morning, two at mid-day and two at night for a total of 3 grams per day to jump start NK cell activity. After three weeks, the dose can be reduced to 1 gram per day (one capsule in the morning and one at night), to maintain the increased NK cell activity level. See the Member Source Directory for purchasing information.

Chapter 4

The lactoferrin miracle

We're on the verge of a major medical break-through with lactoferrin.

Because of this unique extract, much of what we now consider state-of-the-art medicine —such as radiation, antibiotics, and chemotherapy—may eventually seem as primitive as bloodletting.

If lactoferrin proves to be as powerful as it promises to be, many deadly diseases that haunt our thoughts today will no longer frighten us.

Where does lactoferrin come from and how does it work?

From the moment you were born, lactoferrin—an iron-binding protein found in breast milk (colostrum)—was your first shield against infection and disease and your primary source of immune-system chemicals. The primary task of your immune system is to survey your body—organ by organ, tissue by tissue, cell by cell—to make sure that only the cells that are supposed to be there . . . are. When a healthy immune system recognizes a foreign substance—a virus or cancerous cell—it immediately fights to eliminate it.

Researchers discovered the significance of lactoferrin to the immune system while researching another mysterious biological phenomenon: pregnancy.

What's so mysterious about pregnancy?

Until recently, scientists had been baffled by the fact that a woman's body doesn't normally reject a fetus, which naturally contains the foreign antigens of the father. But the puzzle is beginning to unravel: Science has discovered that shortly after conception, a woman's immune system is down-regulated.

This is why her body does not reject the fetus as "foreign" matter. (For this reason, pregnant women should not take lactoferrin.) Immediately after delivery, however, her body produces colostrum, or the first milk, which restores her immune system and provides powerful immune chemicals to the infant. Lactoferrin is the primary immune-system chemical in first milk.

Studies have shown that the mother's first milk is the only source from which an infant can get these significant immune substances. Synthetic formulas can't offer the same nutritional, immunological, or physiological value, despite efforts to produce formulas that mimic breast milk as closely as possible.

Unraveling the healing mystery of lactoferrin

Lactoferrin has at least two specific immune-boosting functions:

- It binds to iron in your blood, keeping it away from cancer cells, bacteria, viruses, and other pathogens that require iron to grow. The lactoferrin protein is able to sequester and release iron as needed, under controlled conditions. This property helps prevent harmful oxidative reactions, making lactoferrin a powerful antioxidant.
- It activates very specific strands of DNA that turn on the genes that launch your immune response. This is such a rare and surprising action that there is no other kind of protein like it. Lactoferrin is in a class by itself.

Lactoferrin also contains antibodies against a wide range of bacterial, fungal, viral, and protozoal pathogens. In effect, the lactoferrin protein backs budding cancer cells or bacteria into a corner . . . starves them and sends out a signal to your white blood cells that says, "It's over here! Come and get it!"

State-of-the-art techniques in cellular and molecular biology have recently allowed us to isolate lactoferrin from the "first food of life." The commercially available preparation is in a form in which the food hasn't been chemically altered.

Widely used to support recovery from malignancies in animals

Numerous studies on rats and patient case histories have documented the benefits of lactoferrin in helping to combat many types of malignancies.[1,2]

Many holistic practitioners use it and achieve great effects by combining it with other immune-enhancing natural tumor-fighting therapies. In one case, a leukemia patient (labeled the worst case the Mayo Clinic had seen in 20 years) had his condition reversed on lactoferrin. His white blood cell count rose, and his problems disappeared. This seemingly "hopeless" case was transformed into a remarkable recovery.

Other case histories indicate that the negative effects of conventional treatments like chemotherapy and radiation are drastically reduced or eliminated with supplemental lactoferrin. (The amounts of lactoferrin used in these reported cases range from

500 to 1500 mg a day.) Again, it should be noted that lactoferrin appears to be perfectly safe, even in high doses.

What else can you use it for?

Other clinical and case studies have shown that lactoferrin…

- contains an anti-inflammatory molecule— which means it can help if you suffer from the pain and debilitation of joint inflammation[3]
- plays a role in lessening ocular disturbance, which means it may help with vision problems[4]
- acts as a potent antimicrobial agent against Candida albicans[5]
- shows potent antiviral activity useful in reducing your susceptibility to viruses, including herpes and HIV[6]

If you're wondering how safe lactoferrin is, remember that it is nontoxic and is well tolerated by nursing infants.

Should you take it as a daily preventive?

There are many everyday threats that wear down the immune system—such as environmental toxins, emotional and physical stressors, and genetic problems. Taking 100 mg of lactoferrin each day at bedtime, however, can help upgrade your immune system, so you can take full advantage of your natural defenses in a world full of potential health threats. For use in cancer recovery, up to 1500 mg a day can be taken without fear of side effects. And unlike penicillin or other synthetic drugs, your body will not become immune to the effects of lactoferrin, because it's something your body is familiar with and knows how to handle.

Since lactoferrin is a natural substance, large pharmaceutical companies aren't able to patent it and make millions. But it's available from a limited number of suppliers in the United States, and it shouldn't be overlooked as a powerful tool in the fight against serious diseases. Lactoferrin can be purchased under the product name of Immunoguard, manufactured by GoldShield Healthcare Direct. For information on purchasing lactoferrin, refer to the Member Source Directory at the back of this report.

Chapter 5

Stop cancer in its tracks with killer grapefruit

Years ago, we published information on MCP's unique ability to stop cancer cells from spreading —or metastasizing—to other parts of the body. But, like many of the products and therapies we cover in Members Alert, at the time, MCP was showing exciting enough results for us to want to bring it to our members right away, but it was also still too new to have much research behind it.

Now, though, there's new research emerging on MCP, confirming its anti-cancer abilities—and shedding some light on just how it achieves these effects. It turns out it's another example of glycobiology, the revolutionary new research field. And this real-life application of that cutting-edge theory is already demonstrating significant results in animal and human trials, against some of the most common—and deadly—kinds of cancer, like prostate, breast, colon, and lung.

Targeting cancer's "getaway car"

MCP comes from pulp and rinds of citrus fruits, like oranges and grapefruits, that have been modi-

fied so that they produce shorter sugar chains. These shorter sugar chains are more readily absorbed through the intestinal tract into the bloodstream, where they can do some pretty amazing things— particularly against cancer cells.

Sugar chains, or glycans, are critical to cellular communications. They bind to molecules on cell surfaces called carbohydrate-binding proteins (CBPs) or lectins and pass along all sorts of information. In this case, the sugar chains in MCP seem to target one very specific lectin called galectin-3 that plays an important role in cancer development.

Studies have repeatedly shown elevated levels of galetin-3 in cancerous tissues as compared to healthy tissues. The galectin-3/cancer link has been found in many forms of cancer, including thyroid cancer,[1,2] gastric cancer,[3] pituitary cancer,[4] breast cancer,[5] and colorectal cancer.[6] Galectin-3 plays a role in a variety of biological functions related to cancer, including tumor cell adhesion, angiogenesis, apoptosis, and metastasis.[7]

Scientists think that galectin-3 accomplishes all of

this in two different ways, each utilizing one end of its protein molecule structure. One end, called the C-terminal end, binds carbohydrate molecules on other cells, allowing cancer cells to adhere to each other and to healthy cells. This process allows cancer to spread, or metastasize.

The opposite end of the galectin-3 molecules is called the N-terminal. When a specific amino acid called serine binds to the galectin-3 molecule in a certain position on the N-terminal end, it triggers a series of biochemical reactions that protect the cancer cell from death, or apoptosis. Scientists believe this is a two-pronged defense: The galectin-3 kills off immune system cells that are attempting to attack the cancer cells, and it also forms a protective barrier around the cancer cells, shielding them from the effects of anti-cancer drugs and treatments like chemotherapy or radiation.[8,9]

MCP clogs the cancer-growth pipeline

So what does all of this have to do with some grapefruit pulp? MCP's sugar molecules block the protein's ability to bind to carbohydrates on other cancer cells and on healthy tissues by binding to the galectin-3 carbohydrate receptor sites at the C-terminal end themselves. With their binding sites all clogged up, cancer cells can't clump together and can't metastasize by adhering to other areas. It's a perfect example of the sugar chain anti-adhesive properties.

But some scientists think there may be even more to MCP's effects on cancer cells. I spoke with Stephen Strum, M.D., a medical oncologist and researcher who co-authored a study on the effects of MCP on galectin-3. He suggests that "parking" MCP sugar chains in galectin-3's C-terminal may also turn off its N-terminal protective response, making cancer cells even more vulnerable.

Dr. Strum explained the theory this way: Imagine galectin-3 molecule's two terminals are like a see-saw. When one end is up, the other end is down; when one end is activated, the other is turned off.

That would mean that when MCP's sugar chains bind at the C-terminal end, the protective effect the galectin-3 affords the cancer cell at the N-terminal end would be turned off.

More research is needed to validate this theory, but it highlights another exciting area of research into galectin-3 and the potential of MCP against cancer.

Slow tumor growth—even kill cancer cells

While we may need more data to validate the see-saw theory, there is plenty of research demonstrating MCP's ability to halt or slow cancer development.

There have been several significant animal and laboratory studies demonstrating MCP's potential to stop or slow metastases and even kill cancer cells. In one study, mice were fed MCP in their drinking water and then injected with human breast cancer cells or human colon cancer cells. In all cases, MCP effectively inhibited tumor growth, spontaneous metastasis, and angiogenesis—the process by which cells develop new blood vessels.

In the breast cancer portion of the study, the tumor volume in mice treated with MCP was less than 1/3 of that of the untreated mice. And none of the MCP-treated mice developed lung metastases, while 66 percent of the untreated mice had tumors on their lungs at the end of the study.

The researchers found similar results in the mice injected with colon cancer cells. The primary tumors of MCP-treated mice were half the size of those in untreated mice. All of the untreated mice developed metastases in the lymph nodes, and 60 percent developed metastases in the liver. But only 25 percent of the MCP-treated mice developed cancer in the lymph nodes and none showed signs of cancer in the liver.[10]

As far back as 1995, scientists saw similar results in rats injected with human prostate cancer cells and treated with MCP. Nearly all of the untreated rats (15 out of 16) developed lung metastases in 30 days, while only 50 percent of the MCP-treated rats (seven out of 14) developed lung metastases. More than half of the untreated rats also developed lymph node tumors, while only 13 percent of the MCP-treated rats had metastases in the lymph nodes.[11]

Effective cancer therapy with no serious side effects

It's an impressive body of evidence. The results seen in these studies rival the effects of many prescription cancer drugs. But what makes MCP even better is that it doesn't appear to have any dangerous side effects or interactions. Fewer than 5 percent of people who take MCP report some flatulence or loose stools, due to its soluble fiber content. This can usually be managed by reducing the dose and slowly working back up to the recommended level. But compared to the toxic side effects of most conventional cancer treatments, these problems are very minor.

Again, it's important to use modified citrus pectin (MCP)—not just regular citrus pectin—to obtain these results; studies have shown that only MCP has the ability to inhibit cancer cell adhesion and impact galectin-3 activity.[12] In fact, nearly all of the research on MCP's effects has been conducted with the same formula.

It's called PectaSol, and it's manufactured by EcoNugenics of Santa Rosa, California. PectaSol was developed by Isaac Eliaz, M.D., M.S.. It's identical to the MCP used in many of the studies cited above.

PectaSol is available in capsules or in powder form; according to Dr. Eliaz, most people prefer the powder form because the recommended daily dosage is quite high. To achieve the recommended dose of 14.4 g per day you'd have to take six capsules three times a day. You can achieve the same dosage by dissolving 5 grams of powder in water or juice three times a day.

If you're fighting cancer, talk to your doctor about adding modified citrus pectin to your treatment plan. It may help your body respond better to the treatments you're already undergoing. Or it may just give your body the extra boost it needs to help fight the disease on its own. Either way, it's a valuable addition to any anti-cancer arsenal. For product ordering information see the Member Source Directory.

Chapter 6

Is it really from heaven above?
The cancer miracle that leaves healthy cells healthy

Cancer treatment has come a long way since the use of mustard gas derivatives in the early 1900s—or has it? When doctors discovered during World War I that mustard gas destroyed bone marrow, they began to experiment with it as a way to kill cancer cells. Although they had little success with the mustard gas, it did pave the way for modern chemotherapy—which involves the most toxic and poisonous substances anyone deliberately puts in his body. These treatments kill much more than cancer cells—they have a devastating effect even on healthy ones.

Sometimes it seems as if only a miracle could provide a cure that's both safe and effective. And a miracle is just what Dr. Mate Hidvegi believed he found when he patented Avemar, a fermented wheat germ extract. Studies have shown that Avemar reduces cancer recurrence, cuts off the cancer cells' energy supply, speeds cancer cell death, and helps the immune system identify cancer cells for attack.

A miracle in the making

Back in World War I, Dr. Albert Szent-Györgyi (a Nobel Prize recipient in 1937 for his discovery of vitamin C) had seen the effects of mustard gas up close and personal and was determined to find a safer alternative for cancer treatment. His goal was to prevent the rapid reproduction that is characteristic of cancer cells. He theorized that supplemental quantities of naturally occurring compounds in wheat germ called DMBQ would help to chaperone cellular metabolism, allowing healthy cells to follow a normal course but prohibiting potentially cancerous ones from growing and spreading. His early experiments, published in the *Proceedings of the National Academy of Sciences USA* in the 1960s, showed effects of naturally occurring and synthetic DMBQ against cancer cell lines, confirming his theory.

But it was then that the science community shifted its focus to killing cancer outright—at any cost. His approach, seen as negotiating with the enemy as opposed to destroying it outright, was cast to the side.

It wasn't until the fall of communism in Hungary in 1989—when scientists were allowed for the first time to pursue independent, personal interests—that Dr. Hidvegi picked up where Szent-Györgyi left off.

But when Hidvegi's funding ran out, it seemed as if the research would once again be set aside. He had no money, he had no prospects, and his wife insisted he give up his research and find a *paying* job.

They were desperate. Yet he did still have one thing at that time—faith. Being a devout man, Dr. Hidvegi prayed to the Virgin Mary for guidance—and an investor.

Miraculously, the very next day a stranger wrote Hidvegi a check somewhere in the $100,000 range.

With that money, he was finally able to patent a technique of fermenting wheat germ with baker's yeast. He named this fermented product Avemar in tribute to the Virgin Mary (*Ave* meaning hail and *Mar* meaning Mary). It became the standard compound for research and later commercialization because it assured a longer shelf life while maintaining its live food status.

Avemar is supported by more than 100 reports (written for presentation or publication) conducted in the U.S., Hungary, Russia, Australia, Israel, and Italy and is validated by the publication of more than 20 peer-reviewed publications describing in vitro, in vivo, and human clinical trials.

Reduce cancer recurrence

Since 1996, over 100 studies done on Avemar have impressed oncologists and cancer researchers. Studies have shown that when Avemar is used as an adjunct treatment, it enhances the effects of the standard treatment agents. It's particularly effective in reducing the chances of cancer recurrence.

In a controlled study, 170 subjects with primary colorectal cancer either had surgery and standard care with chemotherapy or the same plus 9 g of Avemar taken once a day. Only 3 percent of the people in the the Avemar group experienced a recurrence, vs. more than 17 percent of those in the chemo-only group. The Avemar group also showed a 67 percent reduction in metastasis and a 62 percent reduction in deaths.[1]

In a randomized study, 46 stage III melanoma patients with a high risk of recurrence either had surgery and standard care with chemotherapy or surgery plus standard care and 9 g of Avemar taken once a day. Those taking Avemar showed approximately a 50 percent reduction in risk of progression.[2]

In a one-year, non-randomized trial of 43 patients with oral cancer, 21 patients received surgery and standard care while 22 others received the same plus Avemar. The Avemar group showed an 85 percent reduced risk of overall progression. Plus, only 4.5 percent of the patients in the Avemar group experienced local recurrences as opposed to more than 57 percent of the people in the standard care group.

Avemar also reduced the frequency and severity of many common side effects, including nausea, fatigue, weight loss, and immune suppression.

Rejuvenate your immune system

Although Avemar was born out of cancer research, it can also help if you don't have cancer. In fact, since one of its main actions is to keep your immune system operating at peak performance, there really isn't anyone who *can't* benefit from it. The biological state of aging counteracts your immune function, particularly after the age of 40. Many of the symptoms generally associated with simply "aging" are due to the declining ability of the immune system to differentiate between "foreign" proteins and natural ones. When this happens, the immune system not only becomes less capable of resisting infection and cancer but also begins to attack the body's own healthy tissues.

Avemar has been shown to normalize the imbalance in the immune system that results from age and stress. It has also been shown to improve the ability of T-cells to respond to antigens and the ability of B-cells to produce antibodies. And it enhances the functioning of macrophages—the key players in the immune response to foreign invaders like infectious microorganisms. So Avemar supports and enhances overall immune strength, coordination, and function.[7] In a sense, it rejuvenates your aging immune system.

Cut off cancer cells' energy supply

One of Avemar's most unique benefits is that it cuts off cancer cells' energy supply by selectively inhibiting glucose metabolism. Cancer cells love glucose: It fuels the voracious growth and spread of tumors. In fact, cancer cells utilize glucose at a 10- to 50-times higher rate than normal cells do.

Cancer cells that have a higher rate of glucose utilization have a greater chance of spreading. It's on these cells that we see Avemar's most dramatic effects. In fact, the greater the metastatic potential of the cancer cell line tested, the higher the glucose utilization rate and the more dramatic Avemar's effect.

Typical cancer treatments like chemotherapy kill off all cells—cancerous and healthy ones alike. But because of how Avemar interacts with glucose, it can selectively attack cancer cells while leaving healthy cells alone. Studies have shown that it would take a 50 times higher concentration of Avemar than is in a normal therapeutic dose to inhibit glucose utilization in normal healthy cells.

Avemar speeds cancer cell death

The second way Avemar works against cancer is to keep cancer cells from repairing themselves. Cancer cells reproduce quickly and chaotically, producing many breaks and other mistakes in the cellular structure. Because of this, cancer cells need a lot of the enzyme known as PARP (poly-ADP-ribose) to repair breaks in DNA before the cells divide. Without adequate PARP, cancer cells cannot complete DNA replication. When there's no PARP to repair the damage, an enzyme called Caspase-3 initiates programmed cell death.

Avemar has been shown to speed up the death of cancer cells by inhibiting the production of PARP and enhancing the production of Caspase-3.[3]

Researchers at UCLA also showed that Avemar reduces the production of RNA and DNA associated with the rapid reproduction of cancer cells. It also restores normal pathways of cell metabolism and increases the production of RNA and DNA associated with healthy cells.[4]

Undercover cancer cells exposed

Avemar also acts as a biological bounty hunter for disguised cancer cells. Healthy cells have a surface molecule called MHC-1 that tells natural killer (NK) cells not to attack. Virally infected cells don't display this molecule, which makes them targets.

But cancer cells have also been shown to display the surface molecule MHC-1, which means that cancer cells can actually hide from NK cells. Avemar helps the immune system identify cancer cells for attack by suppressing their ability to generate this MHC-1 mask, which allows the NK cells to recognize it as a target for attack.[5]

Children with cancer get a fighting chance

Possibly one of the most powerful studies on Avemar shows its effectiveness on children with cancer. Most forms of pediatric cancer have high cure rates from chemo-therapy as compared with adult cancers, but one of the limiting factors in using chemotherapy to treat children is the infection that can often occur during treatment.

Infection often sets in because chemotherapy kills large numbers of the child's infection-fighting white blood cells and destroys many of the bone marrow cells that produce them.

Doctors aware of the immune-enhancing properties of Avemar wanted to learn if it could possibly prevent the life-threatening infections that often occur in pediatric cancer patients.

A recent study published in the prestigious medical journal *Pediatric Hematology Oncology*, showed that such infections and the fever that accompanies them (called febrile neutropenia) were reduced by 42 percent in the children given Avemar after chemotherapy, compared to those not getting Avemar.[6]

Avemar has this effect because it helps rebuild the immune system, increasing the number and activity of functioning immune system cells. It's clear that, unlike conventional cancer therapy, Avemar does not produce side effects—it reduces them. It also allowed the children in the study to take more cycles of chemotherapy, increasing the chance of a cure.

As toxic as a slice of bread

As dangerous as Avemar is for cancer cells, it won't harm the rest of your body. In fact, according to an independent panel of medical, food safety, and toxicology experts: "Avemar is as safe as whole wheat bread."[8]

In Hungary, where it was developed and is manufactured, it is classified as a "dietary food for special medical purposes, for cancer patients" and is a standard therapy for patients with cancer. It is available as a food or dietary supplement in several other countries as well, including Austria, Australia, Switzerland, Italy, Slovakia, Czech Republic, Russia, Israel, and South Korea.

Avemar is made using a patented process that yields a uniform, consistent, all-natural dietary supplement. Although it is not certified organic, it is free of chemicals and synthetics. According to our contacts at American BioSciences, the exclusive North American distributor of Avemar, there is simply no comparison between their product and other wheat germ products on the market because it is the only one supported by research demonstrating its effectiveness in maintaining normal, healthy cellular metabolism and immune regulation.[9]

But since this is a wheat product, there is the potential for allergic response. Although the process of making the product removes all gluten, the principal allergen in wheat, the product can still come in contact with gluten-containing wheat. American BioSciences says that Avemar should not be consumed by people who have had an organ or tissue transplant, those who have malabsorption syndrome, or those with allergies to foods containing gluten, such as wheat, rye, oats, and barley.

It's also not recommended for people with fructose intolerance or hypersensitivity to gluten, wheat germ, or any of the components or ingredients of this product.

If you suffer from bleeding ulcers, you should stop using Avemar two days before undergoing a barium X-ray contrast examination and resume taking it two days after the completion of the examination. This precaution is necessary because wheat germ contains lectin, which can potentially cause red bloods cells to clump.

If you are currently taking medications or have any adverse health conditions, you should consult with your pharmacist or physician before taking Avemar.

Unique delivery system makes fighting cancer easier—and even tasty

The Avemar product our contacts at American BioSciences offer is an instant drink mix called Avé, which combines Avemar with natural orange flavoring and fructose in pre-measured packets.

As a dietary supplement, the recommended usage is one packet per day mixed with 8 oz. of cold water (or any other beverage containing less than 10 mg of vitamin C). I found that the best way to mix it is to shake it in a closed container. When I tried it, it reminded me of Tang, though it wasn't quite as sweet.

You should consume it within 30 minutes of mixing a batch. Also note that it's a good idea to take Avé one hour before or after a meal and two hours before or after any drugs or other dietary supplements.

If you weigh over 200 pounds, use two packets per day. If you weigh under 100 pounds, only use half of a packet per day. Consult with a healthcare professional for recommended usage levels for children, for guidance on alternative usage levels, and for use in combination with other dietary supplements.

Most people who use Avé daily notice an effect within three weeks, reporting improvements in appetite, energy, and general quality of life.

If you work with your health care professional to use Avé as an adjunct cancer treatment, you should know that it will take a good three months before you will see a change in objective measurements—such as blood markers, CAT scans, MRIs, etc. Although some people reported uneasiness in their stomachs during the first few days of using Avemar, the effect only lasted a few days. No vomiting, diarrhea, or any other symptoms were reported.

Chapter 7

New phyto-miracle beats even drug-resistant cancers—and promises great strides for prevention

Thirty years is a long time. Certainly long enough to win a war-or at least call a truce. Yet it was in 1971 that President Nixon declared his "war on cancer," and today, more than 30 years later, it's clear that we're losing.

Even the medical mainstream doesn't deny this reality. According to the National Cancer Institute, if current trends continue, cancer will be the leading cause of death in the United States by the year 2010. Today, one in five people in the U.S. dies from cancer; in fact, one person dies every 90 seconds. And more than 1.2 million new cancer cases are diagnosed each year.

Sure doesn't sound like victory to me.

Yet the mainstream continues to plod along with the same weapons it's been using since the "war" began: chemotherapy, radiation, and surgery-the old "slash and burn" approach.

What's worse, we're seeing a new wrinklecancer cells that are developing immunity to common cancer drugs, almost in the same way that bacteria are becoming antibiotic resistant. Researchers call them multi-drug resistant (MDR) cancers, and some authorities say that as many as 4 million new cancer patients worldwide will be diagnosed with this type of the disease.

And in 30 years, we've made little progress against the most deadly forms of cancer. Diseases like melanoma, pancreatic cancer, brain cancer-victims of these diseases are still offered little hope and even less time.

Of course, the pharmaceutical companies talk about new cancer breakthroughs all the time. Few of them have had a real impact.

But even when an exciting new drug is in development, one that offers hope to millions, it often comes too late for those who need it most. I can't imagine the frustration of a person struggling with cancer, as they hear and read news reports of a scientific breakthrough that could potentially save their livesbut won't be available for at least five years. All too often, cancer patients don't have five years to wait.

That's why I was so excited to learn about a new natural therapy that addresses all these issues. Research suggests it can selectively kill cancer cells without damaging healthy tissue and can help fight even the most deadly forms of cancer. Studies show it can improve cancer patients' quality of life, reduce pain, and may even make multi-drug resistant cancers more susceptible to conventional chemotherapy drugs. And even better, this powerful therapy shows promise in preventing cancer as wellthe ultimate "cure" for this killer.

This breakthrough cancer killer has the drug biz buzzing

Skeptical? You're not the only one. Even the doctors and scientists that I interviewed for this article admitted that they were wary of the latest "miracle" discovery at first. But when they reviewed the research and saw the results in their own patients, they became believers.

But here's the most compelling piece of evidencethe science behind this therapy is so solid, a Canadian biotech company is in the process of developing a new cancer drug based on the same active ingredients. The drug candidate (for the time being, developers are referring to it as PBD-2131) is in preliminary research stages at a major university-based cancer center. The biotech company calls it a "nontoxic anti-cancer chemotherapeutic" that can "cause apoptosis [cell death] in cancer cells" and is "found to be effective in drug resistant (including MDR) cancers" without showing "significant toxicity."

You can be sure that a biotech company wouldn't invest its time and money in a drug candidate unless it showed some serious promise. But, of course, while this drug candidate works its way through the maddeningly slow approval process, people will continue to be diagnosed with cancer

and people will continue to die of cancer. And even if the trials proceed smoothly, you won't have access to this drug for years. Meanwhile, doctors report that their cancer patients are already seeing results from this natural therapy, living longer, more comfortable lives.

So what are we talking about here? Let me back up a few steps and explain. The drug candidate called PDB-2131 that's under research is based on a "pharmaceutically active phytocompound"in other words, a plant-based substance with medicinal properties. And while the biotech company is working to develop a drug candidate that captures that natural power in a patentable package, it can't patent the actual phytochemical it's based onbut that means the FDA can't hold it up, either.

Locked inside one natural medicine—another, even more powerful, remedy

The phytocompounds we're talking about are called ginsenosides. Recognize anything familiar about that word? Yes, it's derived from the name of the common herb ginseng. But that's where the similarities end. Plain ginseng has never been recommended as a natural cancer fighter. But, like most plants, it's composed of thousands of compounds. In the laboratory, those compounds can be isolated, and that's just how scientists arrive at ginsenosides. These small sub-components of ginseng are glycosides, or plant carbohydrate molecules. Each ginsenoside consists of a sugar and a non-sugar component. The sugar component (the anabolic sapogenin) is what fuels cell growth. So in this case it's the non-sugar element, called the aglycon sapogenin, that we're after.

There are many different types of aglycon sapogenins, all designated by the letter "R"for instance, Rb1, Rc, Rh1, Rh2, and Rg3. Once they're taken into the body, they're broken down into two substances: protopanaxadiol (PPD) and protopanaxatriol (PPT). The breakdown also produces a bacterial metabolite called M1. Scientists believe these three substancesM1, PPD, and PPTare the keys to ginsenosides' cancer- fighting potential.

Just consider these research findings:

R-family ginsenosides may work as anti-angiogenesis agents, blocking new cancer growth. A Japanese study showed that treatment with ginsenoside Rb2 "resulted in significant inhibition" of lung metastases in melanoma-infected mice, as compared to untreated controls. The study suggested that the effects were due to Rb2's ability to block tumor angiogenesis-the development of new blood vessels needed to feed developing cancer cells.1 (Notably, anti-angiogenesis drugs are one of the hottest fields of study in mainstream cancer research.)

R-family ginsenosides may be able to selectively kill cancer cells. A study at Toyama Medical and Pharmaceutical University in Japan found that M1, the metabolic component of PPD, induced cell death in mouse melanoma in as little as 24 hours.2

R-family ginsenosides may be able to reverse precancerous growth at early stages.

Researchers from Kanazawa Medical University in Japan proved that ginsenosides can help halt cancer cell development at a critical, early stage. Scientists have identified five stages in the cell development cycle: G0, G1, S, G2, and M. In this trial, the ginsenoside Rh2 effectively froze the development of melanoma cells at the G1 stage-the period immediately following cell division when RNA and proteins are synthesized-putting an end to precancerous growth.3

R-family ginsenosides may enhance the effects of traditional drugs. A study at the National Defense Medical College in Japan reported that ginsenoside Rh2 enhanced the effects of the chemotherapy drug cisplatin against ovarian cancer cells. Mice injected with human ovarian cancer cells were left untreated, or treated with cisplatin alone, ginsenosides alone, or a combination of the two substances. The cisplatin-ginsenoside combination group saw significantly less tumor growth and significantly longer survival time than any of the three other groups.4 Scientists call this effect MDR-Associated Chemosensitivity Enhancement, or MACE, a promising development for multi-drug resistant cancers.

R-family ginsenosides produce no adverse side effects. In study after study, researchers noted that ginsenosides "did not seem to cause any adverse effects"5; "no toxic effects were observed"6

Powerful stuff. But it's important to remember, not all ginsenosides have this cancer-fighting ability. According to scientists, there are over 20 different kinds of ginsenosides in ginseng, and only the "R family" produces these results. So even though a product's label says that it contains 90 percent ginsenosides, unless it specifies that it contains only aglycon sapogenins -specifically, that it contains

PPT and PPD-it's not going to deliver the cancer-fighting benefits.

These substances come in several formulations-all 90 percent aglycon sapogenin-that include other herbs. The particular formulation used by the doctors I spoke with was Force C-and it contains 90 percent aglycon sapogenins.

Here are some of their stories –and I think you'll have to admit that they're impressive:

Doctor dubs treatment success non-toxic "natural chemotherapy"

Jimmy Chan, N.D., a naturopathic doctor, biochemist, and a trained practitioner of Traditional Chinese Medicine, first learned of Force C in 1999. He agreed to try the product on 15 of his cancer patients who had not responded to other therapy. That was in 1999. Today, Dr. Chan reports, 13 of those patients are still alive.

Since then, Dr. Chan has treated over 300 cancer patients with this product. "I am excited because this is the first natural, non-toxic and yet effective treatment. One could say it is a natural chemotherapy almost," says Chan. He tells another story of a 57-year-old female patient who had tested positive for invasive breast cancer. She had a lump in her breast that measured three centimeters. While she waited for her scheduled mastectomy, she went to Dr. Chan and had 13 intravenous treatments with Force C. After the surgery, the pathology reports on the excised tissue showed only atypical cells, or precancerous cells—no actual cancer cells. "They were only showing slight atypia, meaning they were almost normal," says Chan.

85 percent of patients have less pain and an increased quality of life

Dr. Frank Morales, an M.D. in practice in Brownsville, Texas, has treated about 15 patients with various kinds of cancer with Force C. Typically, Dr. Morales' cancer patients come to him too late– after they have already gone through conventional chemotherapy and radiation and "they have just been beaten to death." But even in these patients, Dr. Morales has seen remarkable effects from Force C. "I can tell you that 85 percent of the patients are getting a good quality of life In all of these patients, the change in quality of life seems to be quite rapid because of the diminished pain and I believe it is related to the activity of cancer. If you reduce the activity, the swelling and pain diminishif you have diminished pain, you have more energy to use positively." In one case, a 58-year-old breast cancer patient was able to shrink metastasized lesions on her liver and lungs after only two months on Force C. Conventional doctors had told this woman they couldn't do any more for her. Dr. Morales estimates that this treatment could prolong her life by three to five years.

Natural therapy tackles even the deadliest forms of cancer

According to Paul Ling Tai, D.P.M., president of Health Secrets USA, the other 90-percent algycon sapogenin formulas his firm produces include Immune C, Herbal C, and Force 1000. All are distributed by Women's International Pharmacy.

In developing and researching these compounds, Dr. Tai has worked with closely with other doctors using them to care for patients. He reports seeing remarkable results in patients struggling with some of the most deadly forms of the disease, like melanoma and pancreatic cancer. Currently he's following a small group of pancreatic cancer patients (who usually live only 40 to 90 days after diagnosis) being treated with aglycon sapogenin at the university cancer center I mentioned earlier. They're all alive several months after their diagnosis and-this is very, very important-all are enjoying a surprising good quality of life.

Other reports suggest that aglycon sapogenin may be effective against many other kinds of cancer, including cancer of the brain, colon, lung, kidney, liver, ovaries, and prostate.

While Dr. Tai is gratified that aglycon sapogenin is showing power against existing cancers, he stresses the compound's preventive properties as well. "In Chinese medicine, prevention is far more important than cureI am not necessarily waiting for people who are dying from cancer. I want to help them also. But it's far more important that researchers using these compounds are able to inhibit and may even be able to prevent cancer."

Perhaps we have won the battle. Next, the war.

Member Source Directory

Modifilan (Fucoidan), Fucoidan Sales; tel: (877)663-3438 or (262)642-3009; fax: (775)201-1257; www.Fucoidan.net. 1 bottle of 90 capsules (90 count) costs US$29.00 plus shipping.

Graviola and **N-Tense** Raintree Nutrition, Inc., 3579 Hwy 50 East, Suite 222, Carson City, NV 89701; tel: (800)780-5902; fax: (775)841-4022. www.rain-tree.com

ImmPower (AHCC) Harmony Co. P.O. Box 93 North Vale, NJ 07447 tel: (888)809-1241; www.theharmonyco.com. US$49.95 (30 capsules-500 mg) plus US$9.95 for shipping.

Immunoguard (lactoferrin) GoldShield Healthcare Direct, 1501 Northpoint Parkway, Suite 100, West Palm Beach, FL 33407; www.goldshieldusa.com

PectaSol, EcoNugenics; tel: (707)521-3370; fax: (707)526-7689; www. econugenics.com; 90 capsules (800 mg each) cost US$29.50 plus shipping.

Avé, Avemar fermented wheat germ extract, Harmony Co. P.O. Box 93 North Vale, NJ 07447 tel: (888)809-1241; www.theharmonyco.com. A box of 30 single-serving packets costs US$199.95 plus shipping. HSI members qualify for a 10% introductory discount.

Force C, Women's International Pharmacy, Nutraceutical Division; 12012 N. 111th Avenue, Youngtown, AZ 85363; tel. 877-896-7050 or 623-214-7100; fax 800-330-0268 or 623-214-7708; call for pricing and shipping charges for individual products.

References

Cancer's kryptonite: HSI panelist tests breakthrough seaweed cancer treatment
1 *Cell Bio Toxicol* 1997 Feb; 13(2): 95-102
2 *Radiats Biol Radioecol* 1999 Sep-Oct; 39(5): 572-7
3 *Eur J Haematol* 1995 Jan; 54(1): 27-33

News of astounding natural cancer killer nearly squashed forever
1 Unpublished data, National Cancer Institute. Anon: Nat Cancer 1st Central Files—(1976)
from Napralert Files, University of Illinois, 1995
2 *Bioorganic and Medicinal Chemistry* 2000;8(1): 285-90
3 *Journal of National Products* 1996;59(2): 100-08

Hybridized mushroom extract destroys cancer cells
1 H. Kitade, et al. 33rd Congress of the European Society for Surgical Research 1998, p 74
2 *International Journal of Immunology* XI(1), 1995, p 23-28
3 *Anti-Cancer Drugs* 1998;9: 343-50
4 *Society of Natural Immunity* 1997, p 56
5 *International Journal of Immunotherapy* XI(1), 1995, p 23-28

The Lactoferrin miracle
1 *Japanese Journal of Cancer Research* 1997;88: 184-190
2 *Cancer Research* 1994;54(9): 2310-2312
3 *Advances in Experimental Medicine and Biology* 1994;357: 143-156
4 *Journal of Ocular Pharmacology and Therapeutics* 1998;14(2): 99-107
5 *Medical Microbiology and Immunology* 1993;182(2): 97-105
6 *Antiviral Research* 2001;52(3): 225-39

Stop cancer in its tracks with killer grapefruit
1 Xu XC, el-Naggar AK, Lotan R "Differential expression of galectin-1 and galectin-3 in thyroid tumors" *Am J Pathol* 1995;147(3):815-822
2 Inohara H, Honjo Y et al "Expression of galectin-3 in fine needle aspirates as a diagnostic marker differentiating benign from malignant thyroid neoplasms" *Cancer* 1999;85(11):2475-2484
3 Woo HJ, Joo HG et al "Immunohistochemical detection of galectin-3 in canine gastric carcinomas" *J Comp Pathol* 2001;124(2-3):216-218
4 Riss D, Jin L et al "Differential expression of galectin-3 in pituitary tumors" *Cancer Res* 2003;63(9):2251-2255
5 Nangia-Makker P, Hogan V et al "Inhibition of human cancer cell growth and metastasis in nude mice by oral intake of modified citrus pectin" *J Natl Cancer Inst* 2002;94(24):1854-1862
6 Guess BW, Scholz MC et al "Modified citrus pectin (MCP) increases the prostate-specific antigen doubling time in men with prostate cancer: a phase II pilot study" *Prostate Cancer and Prostatic Diseases* 2003;6:301-304
7 Fukumori T, Takenaka Y et al "CD29 and CD7 mediate galectin-3-induced type II T-cell apoptosis" *Cancer Res* 2003;63(23):8302-8311
8 Glinsky VV, Glinsky GV et al "The role of Thomsen-Friedenreich antigen in adhersion of human breast and prostate cancer cells to the endothelium" *Cancer Res* 2001;61(12):4851-4857
9 Fukumori T, Takenaka Y et al "CD29 and CD7 mediate galectin-3-induced type II T-cell apoptosis" *Cancer Res* 2003;63(23):8302-8311
10 Nangia-Makker P, Hogan V et al "Inhibition of Human Cancer Cell Growh and Metastasis in Nude Mice by Oral Intake of Modified Citrus Pectin" *J Natl Cancer Inst* 2002;94(24):1854-1862
11 Pienta K, Naik H et al "Inhibition of spontaneous metastasis in a rat prostate cancer model by oral administration of modified citrus pectin" *J Natl Cancer Inst* 1995;87(5):348-355
12 Inohara H, Raz A "Effects of natural complex carbohydrate (citrus pectin) on murine melanoma cell properties related to galectin-3 functions" *Glycoconj J* 1994;11(6):527-532

References

Is it really from heaven above? The cancer miracle that leaves healthy cells healthy

1 "A medical nutrient has supportive value in the treatment of colorectal cancer." *British Journal of Cancer* Aug 4; 89(3): 465-9

2 "Antimetastatic effect of Avemar in high-risk melanoma patients." 18th UICC International Cancer Congress, Oslo, Norway, 30 June – 5 July, 2002. *International Journal of Cancer* 2002; 100(S13): 408.

3 "A medical nutriment study has supportive effect in oral cancer." (unpublished, Márta Ujpál et al) see re

4 "Wheat germ extract glucose uptake and RNA ribose formation but increases fatty acid synthesis in MIA pancreatic adenocarcinoma cells." Pancreas 2001; 23:141-147

"Metabolic profiling of cell growth and death in cancer: applications in drug discovery." *Drug Discovery Today* 2002; 7(6): 18-26

5 "Fermented wheat germ extract inhibits glycolysis/pentose cycle enzymes and induces apoptosis through poly(ADP-ribose) polymerase activation in Jurkat T-cell leukemia tumor cells." *Journal of Biological Chemistry* 2002; 277: 46,408-46,414.

"Fermented wheat germ extract induces apoptosis and downregulation of major complex class I proteins in tumor T and B cell lines." *International Journal of Oncology* 2002; 20: 563-570

6 "Fermented wheat germ extract induces apoptosis and downregulation of major complex class I proteins in tumor T and B cell lines." *International Journal of Oncology* 2002; 20: 563-570

"Avemar triggers apoptosis and downregulation of cell surface MHC 1 proteins in lymphoid tumor cells." Scientific meeting of the Albert Szent-Gyorgyi Medical and Pharmaceutical Center of the Szeged University. Szeged, Hungary, 2000.

7 "Studies for the effect of Avemar on tumor necrosis induced cytotoxicity and on TNF production of immune cells." Institute of Biochemistry, Biological Research Center of the Hungarian Academy of Science. Szeged, 1999.

"Effects of Avemar on the early events of the immune response." Institute of Genetics, Biological Research Center of the Hungarian Academy of Sceince. Szeged, 1999.

"Effect of Avemar on macrophages and microvascular endothelial cells." Scientific meeting of the Albert Szent-Györgyi Medical and Pharmaceutical Center of the Szeged University. Szeged, Hungary, 2000.

8 Letter from James Heimbach, Ph.D. of Jheimbach LLC, 10/28/05

9 Avemar Published Research, (www.avemarresearch.com)

New phyto-miracle beats even drug-resistant cancers–and promises great strides for prevention

1 *Biol Pharm Bull* 1994; 17(5): 635-639

2 *Biochem Biophys Res Commun* 1998; 246(3): 725-730

3 *Life Sci* 1997;60(2):PL39-44

4 *J Cancer Res Clin Oncol* 1993; 120(1-2): 24-26

5 ibid.

6 ibid.

Report 3
The Ultimate Cures for Heart Disease

THE ULTIMATE CURES FOR HEART DISEASE

Contents

Chapter 1

Sugar cane extract rivals popular cholesterol-lowering drugs, without the dangerous side effects

Amid reports of health problems and deaths caused by statin drugs, we've learned that an extract of a commercial crop—sugar cane—can lower cholesterol just as effectively.

As we've told our readers over the past couple of years, cholesterol isn't the primary cause of heart disease...homocysteine levels are. Nevertheless, cholesterol *does* play an important role in coronary health, and any good program for reversing heart disease must address that as well. So you can imagine how excited we were when our researchers discovered that a sugar cane extract could *dramatically* reduce cholesterol levels.

While it's drawn from the same plant that produces table sugar, policosanol doesn't affect blood sugar levels when ingested. Cuban scientists, however, have discovered that it can have a cholesterol-reducing effect[1] without creating the uncomfortable and even dangerous side effects associated with statin drugs.[2,3] Statin drugs lower elevated cholesterol by limiting cholesterol production in the liver, but they also have side effects ranging from heartburn to potentially fatal cases of muscle breakdown. This widely prescribed class of drugs—statin sales topped $14 billion last year—includes the brand names Lipitor, Lescol, Zocor, Mevacor, Pravachol, Prevastatin, and Baycol (which was recalled after being linked to over 40 deaths).

In several studies that compared both cholesterol-lowering methods, policosanol surpassed the performance of statin-drug therapy. One Cuban study compared the effects of policosanol to Pravastatin on patients who had elevated cholesterol levels and were considered to be at high risk for coronary disease. Patients took 10 mg of either policosanol or Pravastatin with their dinners for eight weeks. The group taking statins saw their LDL levels fall by 15.6 percent and their total cholesterol by 11.8 percent. But those in the policosanol group exceeded those numbers, and dropped their LDL levels by 19.3 percent and their total cholesterol by 13.9 percent. **The HDL levels of the statin test subjects remained the same, while the policosonal group increased their HDL by 15.7 percent.** Because HDL cholesterol aids in the removal of fat from arterial walls, an increase in these levels is beneficial.

Thousands of people struggle with cholesterol problems, and the chance of developing high cholesterol increases as we age. As we grow older, our hormone levels drop, making it easier for cholesterol levels to rise in our bodies. Researchers believe policosanol may be a safe method of reducing and regulating LDL. In a clinical trial involving 244 post-menopausal women with high cholesterol, researchers first attempted to bring down elevated lipid levels through six weeks of a standard lipid-lowering diet. When this proved unsuccessful, they gave the women 5 mg of policosanol daily for 12 weeks, then 10 mg daily for another 12 weeks. Researchers found that the supplement was effective in significantly lowering LDL levels (25.2 percent) and total cholesterol (16.7 percent). In addition, the women experienced a 29.3 percent increase in HDL levels.[4]

Extract relieves painful leg cramps

One of the common—and debilitating—side effects of high cholesterol is a syndrome known as intermittent claudication—a cramping pain in the calves. This is often linked to poor circulation and the presence of arterial fat deposits (atherosclerosis). Intermittent claudication occurs only during certain times, such as after walking. Removal of arterial fat deposits has been found to decrease claudication.

Researchers at the Medical Surgical Research Center in Havana, Cuba tested policosanol patients who suffered from moderately severe intermittent claudication. In this two-year long study, 56 patients were randomly assigned to receive either policosanol or a placebo.

Researchers determined if the policosanol was relieving the claudication by conducting treadmill walking tests on each subject before the study and again on 6, 12, 18, and 24 months after beginning treatment. Although both test groups showed some progress during the interim tests, the final results indicated that policosanol had a significant benefit for sufferers of intermittent claudication. After two years of treatment, patients in the placebo group were able to walk a maximum of .15 miles while the group taking policosanol could walk .40 miles before having to stop. The **21 people taking poli-cosanol increased their walking distance by at least 50 percent**. Only five members of the placebo group showed a similar improvement.[5]

And it's possible that policosanol could do more than alleviate the risk of heart disease, circulatory problems, and other ailments commonly associated with high cholesterol...

A possible defense against Alzheimer's

Dora M. Kovacs, Ph.D., a researcher at Massachusetts General Hospital, recently received a $200,000 research grant to study the side effects of cholesterol on the development of Alzheimer's Disease (AD). She found that even normal levels of cholesterol may increase the risk of senility-causing plaques and neurofibrillary tangles in the brain, which are associated with the development and progress of AD.[6]

Dr. Kovacs' research is focusing on the development of drugs that inhibit the production of ACAT, an enzyme that enables cholesterol and other lipids (fats) to enter cells and form solid lipid droplets there. Those droplets can hinder the normal functioning of the cell. They can also increase amyloid beta production, which is associated with the progress of mind-robbing plaques and tangles. When lipid droplet levels increase, amyloid beta production increases...and so does the risk of Alzheimer's. Dr. Kovacs and her research team believe that ACAT-inhibiting drugs are the keys to halting the process of cholesterol and lipid buildup that results in AD. But the related research is in its early stages. Dr. Kovacs plans, but has not yet start-

ed, to test ACAT inhibitors on mice specially bred to have AD. Other researchers have developed a potentially safe class of ACAT inhibitors to treat atherosclerosis. But it may be another five to 10 years before this family of drugs is thoroughly developed, tested, and made available to the public.

There may be an alternative therapy available right now, however. In an interview with Emma Hitt, Ph.D. for the Reuters news service, Dr. Kovacs indicated that several studies have shown that patients who take statin drugs have lower rates of AD and other types of dementia. Cholesterol-lowering statins do not appear to hinder the ACAT enzyme, but the act of maintaining low cholesterol levels lowers the risk of dementia. Since statin drugs can induce serious side effects, policosanol may prove to be a better alternative. In double-blind trials, policosanol produced mild, short-term side effects —such as insomnia, headache, diarrhea, nervousness, and weight loss—in less than 1 percent of test subjects. So policosanol may prove to be an efficacious mind-saver as well as a life-saver.

Caution: Researchers warn that policosanol can interact with blood-thinning drugs. So if you try policosanol (after consulting your doctor), your dose of blood-thinning medication may have to be adjusted with careful medical monitoring. If you would like to purchase policosanol, see your Member Source Directory on page 45. If you're already taking cholesterol-lowering drugs or being treated for any other health condition, you should consult with your doctor before trying policosanol or discontinuing any prescription drug.

Chapter 2

New hope for anyone who has ever suffered a stroke

Tocotrienols not only lower cholesterol levels naturally but also keep the blood thin and flowing freely; furthermore, they have shown the ability to actually dissolve dangerous arterial plaque that can lead to a heart attack or stroke. They are also exceptional antioxidants, protecting cells throughout the body from oxidation that can lead to malignancy or damaged blood vessels.

Recently, the medical community was electrified by a study that led to dramatic improvements in stroke

patients. The study used a special tocotrienol preparation distilled from palm oil, called PalmVitee. This ultra-pure and high-potency formula is produced in Malaysia expressly for use in scientific research. Because of the very limited supply, it has never been available to consumers.

The 50 subjects in this trial had each suffered a first, mild stroke. At the beginning of the study, the degree of blockage of their arteries (measured by ultrasound) ranged from 15 percent to 79 percent.

Without making any other changes to their diet or medications, half of the subjects began taking 240 milligrams a day of PalmVitee tocotrienols; the remaining half received placebos. After 12 months, researchers repeated the ultrasound examinations—with startling results. Among those taking placebos, 40 percent showed a progression of the disease, with increased blockage of the arteries. The other 60 percent were stable: no worse but no better. None showed any improvement.[1]

For those taking PalmVitee, it was a much different story. An astonishing 28 percent had improved: Their arteries were actually less obstructed. Sixty-four percent remained stable, with no further progression. Only 8 percent experienced progression of their disease.

As one research analyst remarked, "PalmVitee may not reverse atherosclerosis in every patient, but it is a very good insurance policy (92 percent effective) against its progression and actually reversed the disease for one in four patients. This is very exciting in light of the lack of available medical options."

How to get PalmVitee

Although the results of this trial were stunning, the findings are consistent with previous research demonstrating the positive effect of tocotrienols on cardiovascular health. However, the unique attributes of PalmVitee may have been a factor in the exceptional outcome.

Other palm-derived products are produced from refined palm oil, from which much of the tocotrienol content has been stripped. PalmVitee, on the other hand, is made from a tocotrienol-rich derivative of the crude oil called PFAD (palm fatty acid derivative). The result is an exceptionally pure and potent product that has not been excessively refined and processed. With further clinical trials on stroke patients still pending, we cannot assume that other tocotrienol products will produce identical results. For ordering information, see the Member Source Directory at the back of this report.

Chapter 3

The link between homocysteine and heart disease

The truth is that cholesterol is NOT the deadly threat you may think it is. Aside from the fact that it's necessary for everything from the production of sex hormones to bile synthesis . . . it does *not* clog your arteries unless it has something to attach to: a tear, a rough surface, a ridge, a sharp turn.

When the homocysteine levels in your blood become too high, the perfect conditions are created for plaque buildup. An amino acid, homocysteine, promotes the growing of smooth muscle cells just below the inner wall of the artery. Multiplying rapidly, these cells create a deadly bulge that protrudes into the artery itself. On this bulge, cholesterol, blood products, and calcium begin to accumulate. These are the blood traps that lead to problems like impotence, poor memory, heart attacks, strokes, and even death. And research indicates that you should be just as concerned—if not more so—over your homocysteine level as you are over your cholesterol level.

Destroys arterial walls

A team of Seattle researchers showed that injections of homocysteine rapidly caused early signs of arteriosclerosis in baboons. The researchers reported that in their test, the cells just beneath the animals' artery walls were mutating and reproducing at a wild rate, and this growth was destroying the arterial walls.

After just one week of high levels of homocysteine in the baboons' blood, 23 percent of their artery walls were lost. The researchers found that the higher the level of homocysteine and the more severely injured the inner artery wall, the more severe the signs of arteriosclerosis.[1]

Homocysteine can kill—if you don't know how to control it

Your body forms homocysteine when you eat food containing an amino acid called methionine, which is present in all animal and vegetable protein. As part of the digestive process, methionine is broken down into homocysteine. As long as certain helper nutrients are present, homocysteine subsequently converts back into one of two harmless amino acids. However, when these helper nutrients aren't present, homocysteine levels become dangerously high.

Research shows that vitamin B_6 is one of the key helper nutrients necessary for normalizing homocysteine levels. In a study at the University of Wisconsin, participants given daily supplements of B_6 (2mg/day) experienced dramatic drops in their homocysteine levels. And at the Titus County Memorial Hospital in Mount Pleasant, Texas, patients given vitamin B_6 were able to reduce their risk of chest pain and heart attack by 73 percent.[2] More importantly, they lived an average of eight years longer than those who didn't take the supplements!

Unfortunately, the typical American diet is low in vitamin B_6 and high in methionine. And because of food processing, it's almost impossible to get enough B_6 in the North American diet.

Recent research has uncovered similar links among homocysteine, folic acid, and B_{12} and has found that you need all three nutrients to keep homocysteine levels down.[3]

Here's what you need to do TODAY!

You can't ensure healthy, effective levels of B_6, B_{12}, and folic acid through diet alone. Americans are so deficient in these nutrients that even the Food and Drug Administration (FDA) and the Centers for Disease Control in Atlanta (CDC) have launched campaigns to increase your intake through supplementation.

Unfortunately, we've discovered that most multivitamin formulas fall short. They simply don't have enough B_6, B_{12}, or folic acid to be effective in reducing homocysteine levels.

There are a number of specialized formulas now available that specifically address the homocystine threat. Check your local health-food store, or, you can try a high-quality supplement called CardioSupport that is based on the latest homocysteine research. Each tablet provides 800 mcg of folic acid, 500 mcg of B_{12}, and 25 mcg of B_6. In addition, the formula includes beneficial components that aid in the metabolism of these crucial heart protective nutrients. For information on ordering CardioSupport, refer to the Member Source Directory at the end of this report.

Chapter 4

The single-ingredient formula rivaling a major class of blood pressure drugs

In many cases, you can control your blood pressure with some simple diet and lifestyle changes. But unfortunately sometimes drugs are necessary. Necessary because some cases of dangerously high blood pressure stay that way no matter what you do to try to lower them. And unfortunately because the only drugs that seem to work come with a nasty list of side effects. So we always keep an eye out for natural hypertension alternatives for those of you who need that helping hand. The latest one to cross our desks is called Vasotensin, a product formulated from a single ingredient that appears to rival one of the leading classes of hypertension drugs—but without the potential risks.

Japanese fish alleviates hypertension

Vasotensin is made from a substance called bonito peptides. That's it—one ingredient. But the manufacturer, Metagenics, claims that bonito peptides have been shown to have such significant effectiveness as a single ingredient that there's no need to add any others. So what exactly are bonito peptides?

Well, in general, peptides are short chains of amino acids. Specifically, bonito peptides are amino acid chains isolated and extracted from the bonito fish, which is a member of the tuna and mackerel family.

Bonito peptides have been shown to inhibit Angiotension Converting Enzyme (ACE) activity. ACE spurs the formation of angiotensin II—a potent compound responsible for blood vessel constriction. ACE also has a negative effect on a substance called Kinin, which lowers blood pressure by relaxing blood vessels. So, in other words, bonito peptides seem to slow down the process responsible for high blood pressure.[1]

Now, it must be some powerful stuff—but I wondered just how it was discovered. It turns out that it was a case of one man's (well, in this case, one industry's) trash being another's treasure.

Fish food finds its way to the research lab

The type of bonito peptides used in Vasotensin is actually a by-product of the Katsuobushi manufacturing process.

Katsuobushi is a traditional Japanese seasoning that has been used in soups and other dishes for over 1,500 years, and it's made from the flesh of the bonito fish. To get a better understanding of how the Katsuobushi industry is connected to Vasotensin, it helps to know a bit about how Katsuobushi is processed. The *Reader's Digest* version goes something like this: the fish meat is heat-treated in water and stirred. The result is the seasoning and the remaining residue. Yet it is from this residue that (typically discarded or used as organic fertilizer) we get this promising compound because one creative (and curious) researcher, Dr. Masaaki Yoshikawa of Kyoto University, decided to take another look at its potential. He discovered that this part of the bonito fish's muscle has strong ACE-inhibiting properties. Apparently, through careful purification and separation, nine active bonito peptides have been identified and sequenced.

But you can't get the anti-hypertensive response by simply eating the bonito fish itself or by eating Katsuobushi.

As Dr. Yoshikawa's research uncovered, there are actually nine specific active peptides that contribute to bonitos' ACE-inhibiting effects. The research I read focused on two of them, one called LKPNM and one called LKP. On its own, LKPNM only slightly inhibits ACE. But when ACE interacts with LKPNM, it gets converted into the peptide LKP, ACE-inhibitory activity of LKP is eight times higher than LKPNM. This unique property gives it a longer sustainable effect; accidentally skipping a dose would not produce a quick spike of blood pressure.

But in order to be "activated," these peptides are dependent on specific enzymatic reactions. The problem is, our bodies don't produce the right enzymes to separate the active parts from the rest of the fish, so the only way to get those blood pressure lowering benefits from the bonito peptides is to have them separated from the fish for you. In other words, you need to take a supplement like Vasotensin to get the ACE-inhibiting effect.

Limited—but promising—results

In a human study out of Japan, researchers tested the anti-hypertensive effects of bonito peptides against a placebo in 61 borderline and mildly hypertensive subjects for 10 weeks. For the first half of the trial, 31 subjects (group 1) took 1.5 grams per day of a bonito peptide mixture. The other 30 subjects (group 2) received a placebo. In the second five-week period, the order was reversed: group 1 subjects took the placebo and group 2 subjects received the bonito peptide mixture. During both phases, the placebo group failed to show any significant decrease in blood pressure. And researchers reported that the anti-hypertensive activity was demonstrated without any side effects.[2]

I also managed to get my hands on a study that showed how bonito peptides stack up to mainstream hypertension drugs. In this study, researchers examined the anti-hypertensive activity of LKP, LKPNM, and Captopril (a common prescription ACE-inhibitor) in rats. The group fed LKP showed an immediate response, but the blood pressure started to go back up after two hours. But in the group fed LKPNM, the anti-hypertensive effect was almost the same as Captopril. And the effects lasted over six hours.[3]

The bottom line on Vasotensin is it has potential. Even though the majority of testing seems to have been done by the manufacturing lab in small, short-term studies, all results were positive and showed no bad reactions. Of course, you should keep in mind that it is an ACE-inhibitor, and with these types of products there is always a possibility of potassium buildup and kidney problems. So you still need to work closely with your doctor to regularly monitor your potassium and blood pressure levels, as well as your kidney function.

The dosage recommendation is two tablets twice daily with meals. See the Member Source Directory at the end of this report for ordering information.

Chapter 5

The silkworm's secret: Ease inflammation and respiratory illness with this enzyme

At some point or another, you've probably seen a nature film showing a caterpillar turn into a butterfly: It weaves a cocoon around itself, and eventually it breaks through the hardened chrysalis, having sprouted wings and changed form almost completely. In the case of the silkworm, there is a specific enzyme called serrapeptase that helps break down the cocoon, letting the newly-transformed moth emerge.

Serrapeptase works by dissolving non-living tissue. This ability captivated researchers around the world, who have subsequently studied its effects in the human body. Some of the claims made about serrapeptase (also known as serratia peptidase) may be stretching it just a tad—we've heard reports that it helps with rheumatoid arthritis, ulcerative colitis, psoriasis, uveitis (eye inflammation), allergies, and may even help fight some forms of cancer. While some of those claims make sense logically, we haven't found enough clinical evidence just yet to tell if they're valid.

But many studies do verify serrapeptase's ability to perform two key functions: it dissolves dead tissue and reduces inflammation. And those functions can ease numerous medical conditions. In human trials overseas, people using serrapeptase have found relief from inflammation, carpal tunnel syndrome, bronchitis, sinusitis, and other ear, nose, and throat ailments. According to one alternative medicine practitioner in Germany, it may even dissolve arterial plaque.

Surgical patients treated with serrapeptase experience rapid reduction of swelling

In Europe and Japan, clinical studies have shown that serrapeptase induces anti-inflammatory activity, anti-edemic activity (the lessening of fluid retention), and fibrinolytic activity (the dissolution of protein buildups).[1] Consequently, physicians and patients in Japan, Germany, and elsewhere around Europe have begun taking serrapeptase to ease inflammation.

In a multi-center study involving 174 patients, Japanese researchers tested serrapeptase's ability to ease post-operative swelling. One day prior to surgery, 88 of the patients received three oral doses of 10 milligrams of serrapeptase. The evening following surgery, they received one dose. Then for the next five days, they received three doses per day. The other 86 patients received placebos. The researchers reported that "the degree of swelling in the serrapeptase-treated patients was significantly less than the placebo-treated patients at every point of observation after the operation up to the fifth day." None of the patients reported any adverse side effects.[2]

Ease respiratory disease in three to four days

Researchers in Italy tested the impact of oral serrapeptase on 193 people aged 12 to 77 who were suffering from acute or chronic disorders of the ear, nose, or throat. In a multi-center, double-blind, placebo-controlled study, subjects took 30 mg of serrapeptase a day for seven to eight days. "After three to four days' treatment, significant symptom regression was observed in peptidase-treated patients," the researchers reported. In particular, the treatment eased pain, fever, nasal obstruction, difficulty in swallowing, and anosmia (reduced sense of smell).[3]

Serrapeptase knocks out carpal tunnel and varicose veins 65 percent of the time

Not surprisingly, researchers have also tested serrapeptase's ability to ease other disorders involving inflammation, fluid-retention, and buildup of fibrous tissue. Carpal tunnel syndrome and varicose veins may seem as unrelated as two conditions could get. But as different as they are, symptoms of both have been dramatically reduced using serrapeptase.

The painful symptoms of carpal tunnel syndrome are caused primarily by inflammation. At the SMS Medical College in Jaipur, India, researchers tested serrapeptase on 20 patients with carpal tunnel. After assessing the subjects' conditions, they instructed the patients to take 10 mg of serrapeptase twice a day for six weeks, then return for reassessment. Sixty-five percent of the patients showed significant improvements. No one reported any adverse side effects.[4]

Fluid retention in and around the veins of the legs causes varicose veins. Researchers in Federico, Italy tested serrapeptase on another 20 people with this condition. The patients took two serrapeptase tablets three times a day (for a total daily dosage of 30 mg) for 14 days. The supplement generated good to excellent improvement also in 65 percent of the subjects. It reduced pain in 63.3 percent of cases, fluid buildup in 56.2 percent, abnormal skin redness in 58.3 percent, and nighttime cramps in 52.9 percent.[5]

Few participants in clinical trials have reported suffering from any side effects from serrapeptase. In the varicose vein study, one patient experienced diarrhea, which was alleviated by temporarily decreasing the daily dosage. In other trials, there have been at least two reported cases of serrapeptase-induced pneumonia. However, patients in both cases fully recovered. Serrapeptase is a blood-thinning agent. Consequently, it may impact anticoagulant therapy and other medications. To avoid any potential complications, consult your doctor before taking serrapeptase. Serrapeptase is available from a number of Internet sources, including the Green Willow Tree in a product called SP-Zyme. Ordering information is listed in the Member Source Directory on page 45.

Chapter 6

Ayurvedic herb fights angina, heart disease, atherosclerosis, and more

Once in a blue moon, HSI uncovers a supplement that does so many things, it's hard even for us to believe it's real. Such is the case with arjuna. The Terminalia arjuna tree is found throughout India, and its bark has been pulverized and used for heart conditions for over 2,700 years. Researchers are now investigating other diseases that may benefit from this Indian herb, but it's already a well-proven cardiovascular "cure."

If you're under a doctor's care or taking prescription drugs for any cardiovascular condition, you should consult with a practitioner before supplementing with arjuna. Because the herb is so potent and effective, the combination of arjuna and drugs may cause too sudden or too severe an effect.

Lower LDL cholesterol by at least 25 percent

Although vitamin E has been shown time and again to be an effective supplement for controlling cholesterol levels, the antioxidant capacity of arjuna outperformed the vitamin in a recent randomized placebo-controlled trial in India. After only 30 days of supplementation with arjuna, the test group decreased its average LDL ("bad") cholesterol levels by 25.6 percent with a corresponding 12.7 percent drop in total cholesterol. The groups receiving either the placebo or 400 IU of vitamin E had no significant change in either measurement.[1]

At SMS Medical College in India, scientists gave 500 mg of arjuna per day to a group of rabbits suffering from high blood-fat levels. After 60 days of therapy with the herb, the rabbits' average total cholesterol dropped from 574 to 217 and their LDL levels dropped from 493 to 162.[2] A group of rabbits receiving only 100 mg of arjuna also experienced lower cholesterol levels, although the drop in cholesterol levels was not as significant.[3]

Reduce angina attacks without the side effects of drugs

More than 6.2 million Americans suffer from angina (chest pain) due to an insufficient supply of blood to the heart. While nitroglycerin is a drug often prescribed for this condition, its effectiveness is reduced with each use. Arjuna, however, can continue to relieve angina regardless of how long it's used.

Researchers at Kasturba Medical College in Mangalore, India, tested arjuna against ISMN (Isosorbide Mononitrate), a nitroglycerin-based drug commonly prescribed for stable angina. While ISMN was effective over a 12-week period, it didn't perform as well as arjuna. The arjuna group had a 30 percent reduction of angina attacks, while the group taking ISMN had a 27 percent reduction. While this is not a significant difference, the performance of arjuna is considerable when you take into account the possible side effects of ISMN—lightheadedness, dizziness, a rapid pulse rate, and blurred vision. Scientists found none of these side effects with the group taking the herb.[4] And, of course, arjuna can be used without fear that it'll stop working when you need it most.

Another study found that 15 stable angina sufferers taking arjuna for three months experienced a 50 percent reduction in angina episodes. A treadmill test administered before and after the subjects took the herb showed that angina symptoms were significantly delayed after supplementation. Subjects also reduced their systolic blood-pressure levels, had a marked decrease in their body-mass indexes —which indicates weight loss—and experienced an increase in HDL ("good") cholesterol levels. The researchers concluded that treating stable angina patients with arjuna was an effective way to relieve symptoms.[5]

Patients with congestive heart failure improve in just two weeks

The New York Heart Association has developed a classification system that helps doctors determine the appropriate treatment depending on the severity of a patient's condition. Classes I and II are mild, class III is moderate, and class IV is severe and sufferers are completely incapacitated. In a recent double-blind, crossover, placebo-controlled study, 12 class IV patients with refractory chronic congestive heart failure received arjuna for two weeks in addition to traditional medication. The placebo term of the trial included only traditional medication. During the short treatment with the herb, the patients were reclassified as class III patients due to improvements in a number of cardiac factors. The results were so impressive that during a later third phase of the study, the same patients continued supplementing with arjuna for 20 to 28 months in addition to conventional medications. Their conditions continued to improve, and they were able to tolerate additional physical effort.[6]

Protect yourself from ischemic heart disease

If heart disease runs in your family and you'd like to take preventive measures, arjuna may do the trick. Scientists gave laboratory rats a supplement containing the herb for 60 days, and after that time gave them isoproterenol, a synthetic chemical that causes an irreversible destruction of heart tissue. Researchers found that pretreating the subjects with arjuna offered "significant cardioprotection." They also found that there was a remarkable reduction in the loss of high-energy phosphate (HEP) stores, a protective factor against ischemia.[7] (Ischemia is a reduction in the supply of oxygen to an organ.)

Keep your arteries flowing free and clear

If the cholesterol circulating in your bloodstream isn't removed on a regular basis, it can deposit on the walls of your arteries. While this happens to everyone to a certain extent, thicker cholesterol deposits reduce the volume of blood flowing through your vascular system and decrease the oxygen reaching your organs. Blood vessels with significant deposits become inflexible and hard, which is why atherosclerosis is also called "hardening of the arteries." This can cause a deterioration of tissues and organs. Your arteries also deteriorate from the accumulation of cholesterol. If left untreated, atherosclerosis can kill you. But arjuna has been shown to turn around this life-threatening condition.

In one study, rabbits were fed a cholesterol-rich diet to create atherosclerosis and then divided into three groups to compare the effects of cholesterol-lowering supplements. One group of rabbits was treated with arjuna while the other two groups were supplemented with pharmaceuticals proven to lower cholesterol levels. In a comparison of all three groups, arjuna was pronounced as "the most potent hypolipidimic agent" and proved to induce "partial inhibition of rabbit atheroma."[8] These findings indicate that arjuna may help prevent the buildup of fat deposits in your arteries and possibly correct the deadly effects of atherosclerosis.

The same herb may fight cancer as readily as bacterial infections

One of the unique benefits of herbal therapies is their adaptogenic property. Many times, a single herb can conquer diseases and medical disorders with seemingly different origins and mechanisms. (Drug therapy is much more targeted and thus limited.) Doctors prescribe antibiotics for bacterial infections and must use completely different types of drugs to fight cancer. Although bacteria and cancer seem to start and spread by different means, arjuna has been shown to successfully fight both.

According to the Entomology Research Institute of Loyola College in India, E. coli, which is a dangerous food-borne pathogen, is no match for arjuna. Researchers tested 34 traditional tribal plants of India and found that arjuna had "significant antibacterial activity" against E. coli as well as the bacteria responsible for pneumonia, cystitis (a bladder infection), and pyelonephritis (a kidney infection).[9]

Salmonella typhimurium is the culprit behind paratyphoid fever, which is a milder form of typhoid fever, as well as salmonella gastroenteritis, a type of food poisoning. But researchers found that ellagic acid, one of the constituents of arjuna, is quite effective against it and stops it from mutating, thus preventing the spread of disease.[10]

While antibacterial drugs have not been proven to work against cancer, it appears arjuna can live up to this double duty—and without the damaging effects of chemotherapeutic drugs. Many of the side effects of prescription drugs, especially those used to treat cancer, may damage organs or have a serious negative impact on general health. But according to studies at the University College of Medical Sciences and SMS Medical College, both in India, researchers have not found liver or renal damage in either human or animal test subjects receiving arjuna.[11,12]

While no one drug or therapy works against all types of cancers, arjuna may help fill in the gap for some forms of the disease. According to scientists at the Department of Botanical Sciences at Guru Nanak Dev University in India, arjuna has cancer-fighting properties and may be a promising agent for stopping cell mutation[13]—believed to be one of the first steps in cancer development. By preventing this initial process, arjuna may cut off one of the most common routes used to convert normal cells into cancerous ones.

In research conducted by the National Institute of Bioscience and Human Technology in Japan, even osteosarcoma, a type of malignant bone tumor, was found to be no match for arjuna. By inhibiting the growth of osteosarcoma cells, arjuna may be able to prevent the growth and spread of this type of cancer.[14]

T. arjuna is not only effective— it's inexpensive!

Scientists still don't fully understand the many disease-fighting mechanisms of arjuna, so research on this herb continues. We've only scratched the surface of this incredible tree and will continue to keep you updated as new uses for it are discovered. T. arjuna is available from Himalaya USA under the name of "Arjuna – Cardiac Tonic." Refer to the Member Source Directory below for ordering information.

Member Source Directory

Policosanol, Life Extension Foundation; tel. (800)544-4440; fax (954)771-2308; www.lef.org. One bottle (60 tablets) for US$24.00 plus shipping.

Palm Vitee CompassioNet; 27 McKee Drive, Mahwah, NJ 07430; tel. (800)510-2010, fax (201)661-6021 www.compassionet.com.

CardioTotal Gold Shield Healthcare Direct; tel. (800)474-9495; www.goldshieldusa.com.

Arjuna Himalaya Herbal Healthcare; 10440 West Office Drive; Houston, TX 77042; tel. (800)869-4640 or (713)863-1622 www.himalayausa.com.

Serrapeptase, The Green Willow Tree; tel. (877)968-4337 or (828)665-3095; fax (208)330-2445; www.greenwillowtree.com.

Vasotensin, Center for Natural Medicine Dispensary, 1330 S.E. 39th Avenue, Portland, OR 97214; tel. (888)305-4288 or (503)232-0475; www.cnm-inc.com

References

Sugar cane extract rivals popular cholesterol-lowering drugs, without the dangerous side effects
1 *Arch Med Res*, 29(1):21-4, 1998
2 *Rev Med Chil*, 127(3):286-94, 1999
3 *Int J Clin Pharmacol Res*, 19(4):117-27, 1999
4 *Gynecol Endocrinol*, 14(3):187-95, 2000
5 *Angiology*, 52(2):115-25, 2001
6 www.ahaf.org/alzdis/research/awards_body.htm

New hope for anyone who has ever suffered a stroke
1 Lipids 1995; 30(12): 1179-83

The link between homocysteine and heart disease
1 *New England Journal of Medicine* 1974;291: 537-43
2 Research Communications in Molecular Pathology and Pharmacology 1995; 89(2): 208-20
3 *American Journal of Clinical Nutrition* 1998;68(5): 1104-10

The single-ingredient formula rivaling a major class of blood pressure drugs
1 *What Your Doctor May Not Tell You About(TM): Hypertension : The Revolutionary Nutrition and Lifestyle Program to Help Fight High Blood Pressure*, New York: Warner Books, 2003
2 Fujita H, Yamagami T, Ohshima K. "Effect of an ace-inhibitory agent, katuobishi oligopeptide, in the spontaneously hypertensive rat and in borderline and mildly hypertensive subjects." *Nutr Res* 2001; 21: 1,149-1,158
3 "LKPNM: a prodrug-type ACE-inhibitory peptide derived from fish protein." *Immunopharmacology* 1999; 44: 123

The silkworm's secret: Ease inflammation and respiratory illness with this enzyme
1 *J Int Med Res* 1990; 18(5): 379-88
2 *Pharmatherapeutica* 1984: 3(8): 526-30
3 *J Int Med Res* 1990; 18(5): 379-88
4 *J Assoc Physicians India* 1999 Dec; 47(12): 1,170-2
5 *Minerva Cardioangiol* 1996 Oct; 44(10): 515-24

Ayurvedic herb fights angina, heart disease, atherosclerosis, and more
1 *Journal of the Association of Physicians of India* 2001;49: 231-35
2 *Journal of Ethnopharmacology* 1997;55(3): 165-69
3 *Journal of Ethnopharmacology* 1997;55(3): 165-69
4 *Journal of the Association of Physicians of India* 1994;42(4): 287-89
5 *International Journal of Cardiology* 1995;49(3): 191-99
6 *International Journal of Cardiology* 1995;49(3): 191-99
7 *Indian Journal of Physiology and Pharmacology* 1998;42(1): 101-06
8 *International Journal of Cardiology* 1998;67(2): 119-24
9 *Journal of Ethnopharmacology* 1998;62(2): 173-82
10 *Indian Journal of Experimental Biology* 1997;35(5): 478-82
11 *Journal of the Association of Physicians of India* 1994;42(4): 287-89
12 *Journal of Ethnopharmacology* 1997;55(3): 165-69
13 *Journal of Environmental Pathology, Toxicology and Oncology* 2001;20(1): 9-14
14 *In Vitro Cellular & Developmental Biology: Animal* 2000;36(8): 544-47

Clogged Lungs Cleared:
Stopping America's 4th Biggest Killer

Clogged Lungs Cleared:
Stopping America's 4th Biggest Killer

When one of our contacts called us about a product he referred to as "truly bizarre," I thought "How 'out there' can it really be?" After all, we come across some pretty unique and complex stuff almost daily in the course of our research. But in this case, there really is no other word to describe the novel treatment for cystic fibrosis, chronic obstructive pulmonary disease, and other respiratory ailments that he told me about: Bizarre sums it up nicely.

It's a liquid formula of DNA called Mucolyxir that, applied sublingually, helps dissolve airway-blocking mucous. That's right—DNA under your tongue to help you breathe better: See what we mean by bizarre?

But not only does it appear to be safe and effective, it also costs much less than you might expect for something this revolutionary.

Ancient theory meets modern science

One of the primary theories explaining respiratory diseases is that much of the mucous blocking the airways is a result of the immune system's effort to eliminate bacteria from the lungs.

Mucolyxir's developers, John McMichael and Allan Lieberman, took that theory and further hypothesized that such activity, over time, could result in hypersensitivity that would exacerbate the problem of mucous accumulation. To address this problem, they turned to the ancient homeopathic concept of "like cures like."

As you'll see below, much of the mucous build-up involved in respiratory illnesses like cystic fibrosis and chronic obstructive pulmonary disease (COPD) is caused by accumulated DNA. So McMichael and Lieberman chose the "like" cure—DNA—as the basis for their Mucolyxir formula.

DNA therapy interrupts vicious cycle

Inside the lungs, the scenario might go something like this: Bacterial-DNA induces the production of various interleukins (such as IL-8), which are associated with inflammation. The presence of IL-8 sends out a distress signal through your body. In turn, responding immune cells attack and destroy the invaders by engulfing them in mucous. But as the immune cells respond, they spill their own DNA, which is interpreted as an enemy invader in the respiratory environment. This sparks another signal for help, establishing a vicious and contin-

ually amplified cycle as the immune cells are repeatedly called into play.

Mucolyxir interrupts this cycle by reducing the production of "signaling" interleukins in order to decrease the production of the protective mucous, which is often more harmful than helpful. It does this in two ways: by regulating anti-DNA activity of the immune system, and by clearing mucous to eliminate matter clogging the airways.

Mucociliary clearance involves the movement of the cilia (the tiny arm-like fibers on the cells lining the bronchial tree), secretion of mucous, and movement of water into and out of epithelial cells. In plain English, that means that the tiny fibers in your lungs are stimulated, causing mucous secretion and movement of water, which, basically, forces you to "cough up" the material clogging your airway. The DNA in Mucolyxir stimulates this process.

The DNA that McMichael and Lieberman used in creating Mucolyxir was extracted from salmon, but it's important to understand that there is no gene transfer with this method of DNA use. In other words, you won't suddenly start showing characteristics of salmon. I spoke to Dr. Lieberman to ask how we can be sure that there's no risk of this happening: After all, you don't need gills or fins.

He explained that Mucolyxir uses a microdose of DNA, meaning that there is not even one full genome present in the product. He pointed out that we eat foreign DNA all the time: When you eat a sardine, you are eating the complete sardine DNA, yet you don't take on any characteristics of a sardine. Fortunately, it just doesn't work that way.

Dr. McMichael noted that, based on his observations, Mucolyxir appears to be "helpful in the treatment of severe respiratory conditions like chronic bronchitis and COPD. People treated with it demonstrate significant improvements in objective parameters such as improved pulmonary function leading to better blood oxygenation efficiency and exercise ability. This product has been formulated to address an unmet medical need that affects a large number of people worldwide."

And that "large number" is growing every day. While cigarette smoke and work environments (such as textile manufacturing and mining) are the most common causes of COPD, it's not just the smokers, miners, and manufacturers at risk. A new generation in respiratory trauma is on the rise, one brought on by irritants like toxic mold found inside-possibly even in your own home. These conditions can lead to cases of asthma and COPD.

While pinning down and eliminating these factors is obviously the best solution, that may not always be possible—especially before the onset of respiratory problems. But the good news is that although the formula was originally developed to treat cystic fibrosis (CF), research also supports Mucolyxir's potential for stimulating an immune response that can protect against or reduce symptoms of asthma and COPD.

Real-world results for conditions from CF to chronic sinusitis

This all still sounds a little like science fiction, but the applications of Mucolyxir are certainly showing real-word results. While it doesn't cure severe respiratory disease, it does make the symptoms more manageable, in turn, improving quality of life. And although there are no controlled clinical trials at this point, there are some remarkable anecdotal accounts.

Consider the case study of 23-year-old twin brothers, both afflicted with cystic fibrosis. Each had a history of hospitalizations for lung clearance and secondary infections diagnosed as being associated with their cystic fibrosis. Each brother began therapy with one or two drops (0.0006 mg/drop) of DNA sublingually per day.

For almost seven years since beginning DNA therapy, neither has been hospitalized. In addition, follow-up evaluations by physicians revealed a 30 to 45 percent increase in airflow in each patient. And that's not all: Forced vital capacity, a common measure of lung capacity, and the extent of mucous clearance in the lungs increased from 60 to 90 percent in each patient.

After approximately one year of therapy, one of the brothers stopped taking the DNA drops. His condition steadily worsened, with increased mucous viscosity, decreased lung capacity, and reduced expectoration. When he resumed taking the DNA drops at the prescribed dose, he immediately improved once again.

Another example of Mucolyxir's potential is that of a 48-year-old woman with chronic sinusitis and bronchitis characterized by chronic head congestion, nasal obstruc-

tion, and coughing. She also began treatment with one drop per day of DNA. After just a few days, she noted a dramatic improvement in sinus and chest drainage. Again, when she stopped taking the DNA drops, her condition regressed. Beginning therapy again caused a similar increase in drainage and relief of congestion she'd experienced previously.

Our medical adviser, Dr. Martin Milner, also told us that people with acute or chronic asthma who have excessive mucus production could also be helped by Mucolyxir.

Recommended protocol

When I spoke with Dr. Lieberman, I also asked him to explain what exactly is involved in using Mucolyxir. He told me that it is administered sublingually (under the tongue) in doses of just one drop at a time.

The single drop should be applied on the floor of the mouth, behind the lower teeth, and you should refrain from swallowing for 15 seconds. To avoid dilution, you should also avoid eating or drinking for five minutes after application.

He emphasized that all patients, regardless of diagnosis, are advised to employ the "rush technique" on the first day of using Mucolyxir. This technique involves taking one drop every 15 minutes for one hour. After the first hour, take one drop every hour until bedtime.

On the second and third days of treatment, take one drop four times daily: one after each meal and one before bed. Beginning on day four, use only as needed—more drops on days with severe symptoms, fewer on good days.

Now, what about cost? A formula based on DNA certainly sounds like it would be expensive. But, at about $35, Mucolyxir is actually fairly affordable, especially considering the cost, in terms of potentially dangerous side effects, associated with the mainstream treatments—like bronchodilators, antibiotics, and even lung transplants—currently used for cystic fibrosis and COPD.

The drops are stable whether they're refrigerated or at room temperature, so you can carry them with you, for quick easy access, in your pocket, purse, or briefcase without worry.

Natural Energy Boosters:

Banish Fatigue and Feel Years Younger

NATURAL ENERGY BOOSTERS:
BANISH FATIGUE AND FEEL YEARS YOUNGER

Contents

Chapter 1

Who wouldn't want 52% more energy: What the "Goldilocks Effect" can do for fatigue and your immune system

We wade through so much dense science every day that when someone came to us recently and wanted to talk about Goldilocks, it was a welcome change of pace. But you'd be surprised just how closely related science and Goldilocks really are—especially when it comes to your energy levels.

Remember her unwavering dedication to finding things that were "just right" for her needs? Well, the new product HSI recently learned about takes this lesson to heart, and, as a result, provides significant relief of fatigue in over 90 percent of the people who try it.

It's called COBAT and it was originally developed by cancer researchers. Unlike toxic chemotherapies that are designed to destroy cancer cells, COBAT, a combination of two amino acids, taurine and beta-alanine, is a type of immunotherapy and is designed to stimulate the patient's immune system into anti-cancer activity. This can be a risky proposition for the patient: Sometimes stimulating the immune system can create other problems, such as allergic reactions or autoimmune disorders. But, in this case, the researchers found that COBAT didn't simply stimulate the immune system, it normalized it. It's actually an immune modulator.

Another way to describe COBAT's effect is "adaptogenic." An adaptogen is a substance that the body uses as it is needed. Instead of having one specific effect, adaptogens allow the body to adapt to various conditions, bringing it into a state of normalcy. For example, an adaptogenic substance that helps regulate temperature wouldn't be limited to making you either hot or cold but would cool you when you're too warm and warm you when you're too cold. COBAT seems to have this kind of effect on the immune system.

Not your average energy booster

And it's these immune-regulating effects that make COBAT so different from other energy boosters.

To combat fatigue, most people choose some type of stimulant, whether it's caffeine, an herbal supplement, or sugar. Those inclined to natural products might buy herbal stimulants, long-distance truck drivers and late-studying students favor mild over-the-counter stimulants, and some folks take their chances by abusing legal or illegal drugs. Overall, Americans spend over $100 billion dollars a year on "pick-me-ups."

But all of these substances generally address one or more of the same mechanisms to alleviate fatigue. They stimulate the central nervous system, which increases blood pressure and heart rate; they stimulate the endocrine system to produce more adrenaline, which, in turn, stimulates the central nervous system; they elevate blood sugar; and/or they alter brain chemistry. These approaches do yield short-term results but often have long-term side effects. They stress the body and can eventually lead to a variety of illnesses-and, ironically, increased fatigue.

COBAT, on the other hand, goes directly to the cause of fatigue: irregularities in your immune system. Of course, that begs the million-dollar question:

What does the immune system have to do with fatigue?

Fatigue can seem to result from a number of causes: blood sugar disorders, chronic infections, allergies, and toxicity. But all of these affect, or are affected by, a group of chemicals called cytokines. Cytokines are proteins produced by various types of white blood cells that make up the immune system. They act as messengers between the cells, enabling them to work together. Cytokines also stimulate cells to produce other cytokines, resulting in "cytokine cascades." Cancer researchers studying the immune system have long known that an increase in certain cytokines can cause a "cytokine syndrome" of fatigue, fever, brain fog, muscle pain, and depression.

At the 38th annual meeting of the American Academy of Environmental Medicine in 2003, Aristo Vodjani, Ph.D., of ImmunoScience Laboratories, presented studies on 2,500 patients with chronic fatigue syndrome, fibromyalgia, and Gulf War Syndrome—all fatiguing illnesses. Dr. Vodjani showed that these patient groups exhibited surprising similarities in cytokine patterns. It appeared that the body, in trying to protect itself from infection and other stressors, established a cytokine pattern associated with lower energy and pain. While it's obviously critical to deal with underlying infections and stressors, it also makes sense to consider balancing the cytokines directly.

This is where Goldilocks comes into the story

Not too many. Not too few. Just the right amount of cytokines.

According to research done at the University of Maryland, COBAT increases the production of some cytokines and decreases others, and this alters existing cytokine patterns that apparently are a major cause of fatigue.

Floyd Taub, M.D., one of the chief investigators, described this as the "Goldilocks effect": Not too much, not too little, but just the right balance of cytokines.

Another member of the research team, Thomas M. Dunn, M.D., noted that COBAT's key effect might be the change in calcium flux it induces. Calcium flux, the movement of calcium ions in a cell, is the primary activation signal for immune cells that leads to an amplifying cascade of immune stimulation under the appropriate conditions.

Safety proven in homeopathic trials

COBAT is basically a combination of the amino acids taurine and beta-alanine. (COBAT is short for the chemical name "carbobenzoxy beta-alanine-taurine.") Taurine and beta-alanine perform numerous biological functions. Taurine helps regulate the heartbeat, maintain cell membrane stability, and prevent brain cell overactivity. Beta-alanine is a constituent of vitamin B5 (pantothenic acid) and coenzyme A, both of which play important roles in various metabolic reactions.

COBAT is similar to garlic, alpha-lipoic acid, MSM, and N-acetyl cysteine in that it contains a sulfur compound. However, while these substances and amino acids are usually administered in doses of up to a gram or more, COBAT's therapeutic dosage is measured in billionths of a gram. To get to those tiny dosage amounts, COBAT is prepared in the same way as homeopathic preparations, diluting it by a factor of 10 six times ("6X" in homeopathic nomenclature).

These miniscule amounts are one reason COBAT is considered nontoxic and extraordinarily safe. One animal study found that rats tolerated 2,000 milligrams of COBAT per kilogram of body weight for 14 days with no adverse effects. The normally prescribed dosage of COBAT is 1 billion times lower than this level. Other animal studies found no signs of toxicity, no increase in mortality, and no abnormal findings when COBAT was administered at thousands and millions of times the prescribed dosage.

In March of 2001, 39 normal volunteers completed the first homeopathic proving trial for COBAT. In this case, the term "normal" means random, in that the volunteers were not chosen because they had specific conditions, as was done for other trials.

The study was conducted by David Riley, M.D., associate clinical professor at the University of New Mexico School of Medicine, editor in chief of the peer-reviewed journal *Alternative Therapies in Health and Medicine*, and co-founder of the Integrative Medicine Institute. The volunteers were given one or two drops of COBAT in 6X or 8X strengths for at least one month.

In this double-blind trial, 92 percent of the patients given COBAT reported significant reductions in fatigue, versus 26 percent of the patients given a placebo. A few volunteers felt better in minutes, the majority felt a difference in days, and a few not at all.

Dr. Riley told me that in all of the trials similar to this one that he's been involved with, "COBAT produced the strongest effects." Another measure of how significant these results are came from Dr. Taub, who verified the significance of these results, saying that "standard allopathic treatments for fatigue are effective less than half of the time." But, as mentioned before, those positive effects come complete with a variety of side effects and compromises—unlike COBAT.

Trials show a number of other benefits

Reduced fatigue was not the only benefit found in the homeopathic trial. Other symptoms addressed by COBAT in this study included appetite abnormalities, coughs and colds, headaches, digestive problems, uterine fibroids, headaches and muscle aches, neurological problems, and premenstrual syndrome (PMS).

One patient, a 55-year-old female with lung cancer, entered the study for fatigue and allergies. In addition to less fatigue and less frequent and severe allergy symptoms, she reported that COBAT helped with her recovery from chemotherapy by helping to maintain her appetite and weight.

In a trial held in 2002, all but one of 16 patients diagnosed with cancer, hepatitis C, or chronic fatigue syndrome reported significant improvements. COBAT was four to 10 times more effective than conventional drug therapies in reducing fatigue in CFS patients. The rest of the subjects reported an average 52 percent improvement in their energy levels. There were no other interventions or changes in diet and activities, and about half of the improvement was noted within four to 10 weeks.

Again, patients reported positive effects on other health complaints, citing improvement in memory, and decreases in depression, headaches, allergies, pain, and gastrointestinal symptoms. Several patients also entered the trial with elevated liver enzymes, a sign of liver disease. All of their readings decreased to normal during the trial.

Effective against mild fatigue in healthier people

Normally, we should experience fatigue only as a sign that it's time to go to sleep, after extraordinary physical or mental exertion, or when we have serious health conditions, like the patients in the studies outlined above. These days, however, fatigue affects many of us even when we seem to be in otherwise good health. Everyone wants more energy, and COBAT appears to be unequaled in its effectiveness, safety, and ancillary benefits.

So after all the formal results were in, Stephen Levine, president of the Allergy Research Group, was curious about how COBAT would work on people who are generally healthy but describe themselves as having "mild" fatigue. He recruited a few friends and co-workers to try COBAT. These anecdotal comments don't compare to the scientific evidence, of course, but they are interesting.

A co-worker with fibromyalgia said that after five days on COBAT, she "awoke feeling like a completely different person." Her twin sister, who has chronic pain from an unsuccessful shoulder operation, said "after two weeks, I started waking up feeling refreshed and had a better ability to concentrate." A menopausal woman

noted that COBAT "decreased brain fog and increased my mental clarity...I slept soundly and awoke refreshed and relaxed." And one person (lucky enough to have no health complaints), said "COBAT...creates no buzz or edginess, yet it provides energy for both physical and mental work. It allowed me to stop drinking caffeinated coffee for the first time in my adult life."

Where to get COBAT and how to use it

COBAT is sold under the brand name Taurox 6X. While the full dose is 12 drops daily, many of the test participants gained full benefits with less. In fact, the label suggests trying "half or even fewer drops." If you do, you can stretch a half-ounce bottle into more than a one-month supply.

Dr. Levine told me that "each patient should determine his or her best dose—the fewest drops that produce the desired benefit without any symptoms." He went on to comment that patients who start with the 6X who get headaches or find themselves with "too much energy" should use fewer drops.

The manufacturer warns that Taurox 6X should not be taken with immunosuppressive agents, or by patients who have had an organ transplant. People with autoimmune diseases should consult with their doctors before using it.

Because of a lack of testing, Taurox 6X is not recommended for pregnant or nursing women or children under 15.

Taurox does run on the expensive side: The 6X preparation averages about $47 for 13.5 ml. (See the Member Source Directory on page 59 for complete ordering information.) But keep in mind that, as an adaptogen, odds are it might help improve other aspects of your health too, by regulating your immune system's cytokine levels. In other words, Taurox could go a long way in helping you reach your own personal "just right." Goldilocks would be proud.

Chapter 2

Erase debilitating pain and fatigue by recharging your cells' batteries

Low energy is probably the No. 1 complaint I hear from my patients. But in many cases, the underlying problem may be more serious than "just getting older." It can actually reflect reduced energy in the cells, much like a battery wearing down and needing to be recharged. And the key to boosting

cellular energy is to provide the cells with the fuel they need to function at peak performance, the enzyme adenosine triphosphate (ATP). How? With a simple five-carbon sugar found in every cell of the body called D-ribose, or simply "ribose," the cellular battery recharger.

Ribose's main function is to regulate the production of ATP—the major source of energy for all your cells. This action makes it useful for all sorts of conditions, including heart disease, congestive heart failure, and fibromyalgia. It's even good for supplying extra energy for workouts, and restoring energy after sustained exertion.

Ribose can be made naturally in the body, but it's a slow process limited by several enzymes that are lacking in heart and muscle cells. There are no foods containing ribose in any substantial amounts. Still, under normal circumstances getting enough ribose isn't a problem. But when the heart or our muscles are challenged from stress or lack of oxygen for any number of reasons, they need an extra ribose boost to restore ATP levels.

The problem, until recently, was that the manufacturing processes for making ribose were so expensive that supplements just weren't a practical—or even feasible—solution for many people. Now, though, there is new technology for ribose production, and the resulting formula, called Corvalen M, offers simple solutions for many people who just didn't have options before.

Two weeks of treatment erases debilitating pain and fatigue

Take fibromyalgia for example. It's often difficult both to diagnose and to treat.

Until now, there have been few tools to help these patients. However, we've found that ribose can provide significant improvement, as seen in the following case study published last year in the journal *Pharmacotherapy*.[1]

At 37, Kris, a veterinary surgeon and researcher at a major university, became so debilitated from fibromyalgia she had to give up her practice.

But then she joined a clinical study on fibromyalgia and began taking 5 grams of ribose two times per day (10 grams per day). Within a week, she felt better. Within two weeks, she was back at work in the operating room.

Over the course of the following month, she continued to improve. After a month, however, Kris stopped her treatment. Ten days later, she was totally debilitated again and could no longer perform surgery. So she began ribose treatment for a second time, again with dramatically positive results, and has remained symptom-free as long as she takes the supplement regularly.

While there's no official explanation as to why ribose is so effective for fibromyalgia, it could go back to its roots in ATP production. People with fibromyalgia have lower levels of ATP and a reduced capacity to make ATP in their muscles.[2] The effect of ribose on the production of ATP may be the link to reducing the strain in affected muscles and allowing patients to return to their previously active lifestyles.

There are other nutrients that, like ribose, are necessary for ATP production. One is malic acid, which also helps to combat fibro-myalgia's chronic muscle soreness. I have been recommending it along with magnesium to my fibromyalgia patients for years with relatively good success. But adding ribose has sparked even better results. Corvalen M, mentioned earlier, combines all three nutrients into one powdered formula, lending a much-needed touch of simplicity to this complicated disease.

Ribose gets to the heart of the matter

I've seen similarly remarkable results in people with heart problems. Heart disease, heart attack, heart surgery, and organ transplants can all lead to restricted blood flow, called ischemia in which your cells don't get the oxygen they need to properly burn ATP for energy.

In addition, individuals who are on inotropic drugs to make the heart beat harder then have an additional strain on the heart's energy production.

So it is especially important that patients with congestive heart failure, chronic coronary artery disease, or cardiomyopathy take extra ribose to offset their energy-draining effects.

Research shows that supplementation with ribose can offset this energy drain without interfering with the effects of any other medication the person might be taking.

Side-effect free at 12 times the standard dose

One of the best parts of the ribose story is that, despite it's being so powerful, it has almost no side effects, with thousands of patients having taken ribose in doses up to 60 grams per day.

How can we be so sure that ribose is safe? Well, first, ribose is made naturally by the body and works with the body's own chemistry. Glucose, the main sugar of the body, is converted to ribose in the cells. Corvalen M contains Bioenergy RIBOSE™, which is chemically identical to the ribose made by the body from glucose. Second, the amount of ribose recommended for supplementation is very small: only about 5 grams one to three times per day. And finally, there's virtually no chance of over-supplementation: Your body safely eliminates what it doesn't need. The only warning I give patients is that it may cause over-stimulation if taken too close to bedtime. In that case, I recommend that they take it earlier in the day, i.e. not past 4 p.m.

How much ribose should you take?

No matter what end of the health spectrum you're on, ribose may help restore energy levels. To keep cellular ATP levels at their highest, ribose should be taken daily.

Maintenance doses of 1 to 5 grams per day should be enough to maintain normal ATP levels. Corvalen M comes in a powder form than can be mixed with water: 5 grams is about 1 teaspoonful of the powder.

If you're concerned about your cardiovascular health, you may want to take more—perhaps 5 to 10 grams per day. However, you should try the lower dosage first and increase as needed. For fibro-myalgia sufferers, I recommend 5 grams two or three times daily. For you athletes: To supercharge your workout and recovery, take 5 grams before and afterwards.

Although ribose is a sugar, for those of you watching their carbohydrate intake, including diabetics, ribose does not act like glucose in raising blood sugar. In fact, it causes a brief dip in glucose, which then normalizes.

So whether you have fibromyalgia, cardiac problems, low energy, or simply want to enhance your workouts, you can recharge your cellular batteries with Corvalen M's special combination ribose formula.

Hyla Cass, M.D., is Assistant Clinical Professor at UCLA School of Medicine and author of several books including *Natural Highs: Supplements, Nutrition and Mind-Body Techniques* (with Patrick Holford) and *8 Weeks to Vibrant Health: A Woman's Take-Charge Program to Correct Imbalances, Reclaim Energy, and Restore Well-Being*. She also serves on the board of Vitamin Relief USA, which provides daily nutritional supplements to at-risk children across the country. For more information see www.drcass.com.

Chapter 3

Human Growth Hormone—the end of aging? New discovery eliminates the risks and lowers the cost of this potent anti-aging therapy

Judging from the thousands of books and articles on "youth" hormones like DHEA and melatonin, you might never guess that these supplements are relatively minor players in the emerging field of longevity medicine. In truth, these hormone-replacement strategies, while useful and effective, pale in comparison to the anti-aging power of human growth hormone (HGH). Benefits of HGH replacement therapy include:

- increased muscle mass
- decreased body fat
- reduced LDL cholesterol
- restored hair growth
- increased endurance
- upgraded immune function
- improved sexual response
- improved skin texture and elasticity

But you won't find bottles of HGH lining the shelves at your local health-food store. Scientists haven't been able to harness the undeniable power of this anti-aging wonder in a way that's both safe and effective—or even affordable—until now.

Scientists at the cutting edge of age-extension research have uncovered new strategies that allow you to enjoy the age-reversing, energy-enhancing, disease-fighting power of human growth hormone, without dangerous side effects and at a fraction of the cost of risky hormone injections.

What is growth hormone?

Human growth hormone, also known as *somatotropin*, is produced by your pituitary gland in response to signals from the hypothalamus gland. High levels of growth hormone stimulate the growth and maintenance of bone tissue and muscle mass. Growth hormone also facilitates the repair of damaged DNA within the cell, as well as proper cell division. In this way, growth hormone may hold the key to slowing and reversing the aging process.

Most of the beneficial effects of growth hormone are achieved through the actions of a chemical called insulin-like growth factor-1 (IGF-1). IGF-1 is produced throughout the body in response to the presence of growth hormone, and acts to enhance and correct intra-cellular communications and function.

Are you in somatopause?

As with hormones like testosterone and DHEA, the level of growth hormone in the blood drops dramatically as you age. The decline starts at around age 30, and by the time you are in your 60s or 70s, your growth hormone levels may be practically undetectable, a state sometimes referred to as *somatopause*.

Somatopause corresponds almost exactly with most of the outward manifestations of aging—sagging skin, waning muscles, hair loss, bone loss, reduced energy, poor memory, reduced sex drive, etc.

Scientists have repeatedly shown that therapies that increase the level of circulating growth hormone can reverse the signs of aging that accompany somatopause. The challenge has been to find growth-hormone replacement therapies that are both safe and affordable.

20 years of aging reversed in six months

It all started in 1990, when Dr. Daniel Rudman stunned the world by reporting in *The New England Journal of Medicine* that he had reversed "10 to 20 years of aging" in 12 elderly men by injecting them with human growth hormone.

Dr. Rudman had been injecting his subjects with HGH three times a week for six months. In that time, their body fat was reduced by an average of 14 percent and their lean muscle mass increased by almost 9 percent. Their skin grew measurably thicker and more youthful looking, and they reported more energy and an increased sex drive.

In the seventh month of injections, however, the first warning bells went off. Several subjects developed debilitating carpal tunnel syndrome—the growth hormone was apparently stimulating unregulated growth of the cartilage in the wrist. Others developed severe arthritis, high blood pressure, congestive heart disease, and diabetic-type conditions. Although the side effects diminished when the drug was discontinued, so did the benefits.

But by that time, there was no stuffing the genie back into the bottle. Rudman's research unleashed a worldwide furor over growth hormone as the quintessential youth drug.

Subsequent studies verified both the benefits and the risks observed in Rudman's original study. Supplementing with HGH consistently results in increased muscle mass, decreased body fat, restored hair growth, upgraded immune function, increased endurance, and improved sexual response. It also invariably produces a list of side effects.

Growth-hormone injections might increase your risk of cancer

One of the ways that growth hormone works is to stimulate the turnover of the body's cells. The fear is that it could also disarm the mechanism by which the body prevents the uncontrolled cell division that allows tumors to form. Some studies have observed an increase in cancerous tumor growth with the use of HGH.

We already know that among children who receive HGH as a treatment for growth disorders (the only FDA-approved use of HGH), the incidence of leukemia is double that of the normal population.

In his 1997 book *Grow Young with HGH*, Ronald Klatz (president of the American Academy of Anti-Aging Medicine) lists some 30 physicians who "specialize" in anti-aging medicine and who will provide growth hormone to those who can afford it—the price tag is about $1,000 a month. For most people, the costs—in both monetary and health terms—are simply too high.

And there's no denying that those with higher levels of growth hormone look and feel younger and healthier. Now, we've uncovered a brand new product that has been proven to deliver the anti-aging benefits of growth hormone, without the expense and risks of dangerous drug therapies.

Preventing "somatopause"—An all-natural therapy to reverse aging

Many people assume that the body's *production* of growth hormone slows as we age. But as researchers James Jamieson and L.E. Dorman, D.O. explained in a groundbreaking presentation before the American College for Advancement in Medicine (ACAM) in 1997, your pituitary gland <u>continues to produce human growth hormone well into your 70's and even into your 80's</u> (unless you have a pituitary disorder).

But as you age, a number of factors begin to interfere with your body's ability to release its supply of growth hormone into the bloodstream. To make matters worse, the tissues of the body become increasingly insensitive or resistant to what little growth hormone is still circulating.

Jamieson and Dorman have focused their research on substances called secretagogues—natural substances that aim to reverse somatopause by stimulating the release (or secretion) of growth hormone. Through painstaking experimentation, they have identified several natural compounds that together appear to greatly enhance the body's utilization and production of growth hormone.

This unique sectretagogue formula is called Symbiotropin. It contains no human growth hormone—or any other hormone. Instead, it contains safe biological *activators* (including specific amino acids, proteins, and botanical extracts) that, by stimulating certain receptors in the pituitary and hypothalamus glands, help your body release its sequestered stores of growth hormone.

The effect mimics (or exceeds) the benefits of HGH

injections: You'll likely experience a decrease in body fat, improvement in skin texture, lowered cholesterol levels, sharper vision, improved memory, enhanced sexual performance, and increased energy —in short, all the benefits of growth hormone therapy—but minus the high risk of complications and the $1,000 price tag.

A potent anti-aging therapy that's absolutely safe—and proven effective

In a study of 36 people, scientists evaluated the effectiveness of Symbiotropin by measuring the levels of IGF-1, a signal that growth hormone is active in the body. Over 12 weeks, IGF-1 levels increased by an average of 30 percent.

But study participants were already convinced, reporting improved energy, endurance, and body composition after only four weeks. After eight weeks, the subjects reported new hair growth, restoration of hair color, and improved skin texture and tone. No side effects were observed.

Doctors who have been using Symbiotropin in their practices are also reporting phenomenal results. Some indicate that it has been three to four times *more effective* than growth-hormone injections! Part of the reason lies in the fact that Symbiotropin mimics the action of the pituitary gland much more closely than growth-hormone injections.

As we've said, HGH works by stimulating the production of IGF-1. But HGH has an extremely short half-life—after being secreted, it is cleared from the blood in as little as 20 minutes! Injections create huge spikes in HGH in the blood, but their effectiveness is limited by the amount of IGF-1 that can be produced in the short window of opportunity before the hormone is metabolized away.

Symbiotropin, in contrast, stimulates smaller, more frequent rises in growth-hormone levels, resulting in steadier elevations in IGF-1. Another significant advantage of Symbiotropin is that it does not suppress the body's own production of HGH (as hormone injections do). In fact, the formulation actually increases your own natural production of the hormone in addition to facilitating its release into your system.

Here are a few of the case histories we reviewed:

J.M., female, age 71: Lost 3 pounds a week throughout a 12-week period. The patient reported increased energy, along with diminished wrinkles and age spots.

L.C., female, age 48: History of severe high blood pressure. With Symbiotropin, she was able to discontinue several medications, including an ACE inhibitor. The patient reports increased energy and an increased sense of wellbeing.

L.J., male, age 55: The patient was overweight and suffered reduced sexual potency. With Symbiotropin, he lost weight and reports significant improvement in sexual potency.

Symbiotropin is formulated in effervescent tablets, which can be dissolved in water and taken on an empty stomach, preferably at bedtime, early in the morning, or 1/2 hour prior to exercise, as directed on the label. After each three-month cycle, you should take a two- to four-week break before resuming.

You will optimize the benefit if you maintain a low-carbohydrate diet, which helps keep insulin levels low. Insulin directly suppresses the action of HGH. For the same reason, you should also avoid taking vanadyl sulfate or chromium supplements (which act similarly to insulin in the body) within two hours of taking Symbiotropin.

Member Source Directory

Taurox 6X (COBAT), Nutricology; tel. (800)545-9960 or (510)263-2000; fax (510)263-2100; www.nutricology.com. A 13.5 ml bottle of Taurox 6X costs US$47.00 plus shipping.

Corvalen M, Valen Labs Inc., ph. (866)267-8253. A 12-oz. jar of powder is US$69.95 plus shipping. Mention Dr. Cass' article to receive a $20 discount on your first order.

Symbiotropin, Center for Natural Medicine Dispensary; tel. (888)305-4288 or (503)232-0475; fax (503)232-7751; www.cnm-inc.com. One box of 40 effervescent tabs costs US$75.00, three boxes costs $210.00, plus shipping.

References

Erase debilitating pain and fatigue by recharging your cell batteries
1 Gebhart B, Jorgenson JA. "Benefit of Ribose in a Patient with Fibromyalgia." *Pharmacotherapy* 2004; 24(11): 1,646-1,648
2 Bengtsson A, Henriksson KG "Reduced high-energy phosphate levels in the painful muscles of patients with primary fibromyalgia." *Arthritis Rheum* 1986; 29: 817-821

Boost Bone Density 27%:
Today's Top Medicines for Women

BOOST BONE DENSITY 27%:
TODAY'S TOP MEDICINES FOR WOMEN

Contents

Chapter 1

The milk-less secret to preventing osteoporosis

In October 2004, the U.S. Surgeon General released the first-ever report on bone health—and the news wasn't good. Apparently, by 2020, half of all Americans over age 50 will be at risk for low bone density and osteoporosis. But this dire warning did come with a silver lining: The risk will only increase that much if no one takes any immediate action to protect her bones.

No problem—we can all handle taking action. It's figuring out what action to take that can present a challenge. Of course, there are the prescription drugs like Fosamax, designed to build bone mass, and the dairy industry still clings to its claim that milk builds strong bones.

But osteoporosis drugs come with their own risks like nausea, altered sense of taste, and bone or joint pain. And milk just doesn't cut it in terms of bone health: In fact, studies show it's not the best source of calcium, the most crucial bone-health nutrient, and it doesn't actually protect against fractures or other bone problems.

You may have already made the switch over to calcium supplements to protect yourself from bone loss and osteoporosis. The key to keeping your bones strong and healthy is to regulate the calcium in your body. And now there's an all-natural product that can help you do that.

It's called Osteophase, and preliminary studies show that it can reduce the loss of calcium, increase bone density, and increase bone remodeling.

Calcium regulating superstars that will save your bones

Osteophase is the first nutritional supplement that reliably regulates calcium homeostasis to rebuild skeletal bone and resolve calcium overload.

It's a marine-based formula made from oyster shell lining combined with 21 different amino acids, iron, zinc, and three specific herbs—stragalus, Angelica sinensis root, and Coix seeds.

The inner lining of the oyster shell contains biologically active proteins and enzymes that are responsible for stimulating the formation of the hard outer shell from available calcium. The manufacturers of Osteophase developed a method of extracting these bioactive ingredients from the shell lining, along with calcium from the actual shell.

When they're combined with the three herbs in the formula, the active components of the oyster shell lining help regulate the functions of calcium in the body, pulling it out of soft tissues where it can cause damage, and re-directing it into the bones to strengthen them.

Research has shown that Astragalus extracts inhibit bone loss in rats that have had their ovaries removed. This could indicate that it may be a good bone-protecting alternative for post-menopausal women who were counting on hormone replacement therapy for this purpose.

Angelica sinensis is frequently used as the main ingredient in herbal prescriptions for bone injuries. One study found that Angelica stimulated synthesis of a substance called OPC-1, which is a crucial part of bone formation.

Coix seeds help counteract the degeneration of bone and cartilage.

For once you need even less than the "experts" recommend

The dose of Osteophase used in the clinical evaluation in China contained less than 125 mg per day of calcium. This level of calcium intake is actually far below the 1,000 mg of daily supplementation recommended by U.S. health authorities to protect against bone loss. But despite the lower level of calcium, the researchers found that Osteophase reduced the loss of calcium by up to 69 percent, increased bone density by 27 percent, and increased bone remodeling by 100 percent.

These results support the notion that Osteophase achieves its results by regulating the amount of calcium in the body—not by increasing it.

So even though the U.S. government probably won't add it to its list of ways to head off the burgeoning epidemic of osteoporosis and bone loss, it certainly looks as if Osteophase might be one of the best tools for taking that "immediate action" the Surgeon General recommended. See the Member Source Directory on Page 66 for ordering information.

Chapter 2

Replenish your body's supply of this natural moisturizer and say goodbye to wrinkles and joint pain

The promotional material reads like an Oil of Olay commercial: "Reduce wrinkles and visible signs of aging" with a dietary supplement used by the porcelain-skinned beauties of Japan. Yes, natural medicine—that wholesome realm of herbalists, naturopaths, and health nuts—has gone "glam" and produced a "cosmaceutical."

But heck, if natural medicine can generate products that boost the immune system, lower cholesterol, and ease hypertension, why can't it formulate products that combat wrinkles too?

A new wave of supplements containing hyaluronic acid—a complex carbohydrate that has been described as "nature's moisturizer"—are purporting to nurture smoother, younger skin. And anecdotal evidence suggests they may also support more limber, less painful joints. Further, some limited clinical experience indicates that hyaluronic acid supplements prevent bruising and accelerate wound healing—a property that benefits diabetics in particular.

But overwhelmingly, HA is a beauty supplement. Over the years at the HSI Symposia, we've met some of the youngest 70-, 80-, and 90-year-olds you can imagine. And since a lot of you let us know that you want to look as young as you feel, we decided to digress from our usual roster of stories about hardened arteries, cancer threats, and liver disease, and devote a few pages to the pursuit of youth—naturally.

The key here is *naturally*. There are plenty of ways to get rid of wrinkles, but whether those products and procedures are safe is another issue entirely. The newest trend involves injecting the toxic substance (an FDA-approved toxic substance, but toxic nonetheless) Botox, into the face. Despite the obvious dangers associated with injecting poison into the body, women around the country have started to abandon Tupperware and bridge parties for Botox parties. We kid you not. Women are inviting friends over to have a strain of the botulism virus, which literally paralyzes the muscles, injected below their eyes, around their mouths, anywhere they have wrinkles—all while munching on chips and salsa and gossiping about the neighbor's affair. We were, quite frankly, very disturbed by this trend and decided to explore a natural alternative. We found one in hyaluronic acid (HA).

When was the last time someone told you how "Toki" you look?

There is actually some science and research to demonstrate that hyaluronic acid can help you look younger. To get to the science, we had to get past a lot of the cosmetic-counter-style marketing lingo. But we just can't move on without sharing a taste of it. Toki, for example, is a multiple-ingredient beauty supplement that includes HA. In Japanese, *Toki* means "skin of a porcelain doll," writes the product's North American distributor, Lane Labs. "The highest compliment a woman can receive in Japan is that she is looking Toki."

Nobody said beauty comes easily. To understand how HA can foster younger skin (and produce a few other health benefits) you first have to understand how your skin, joints, and soft tissue function at a cellular level. It's a little complicated. One senior educator with a formulating company told us that she has a particularly difficult time educating sellers about her HA supplement simply because the science behind HA is so much more complicated than the science behind a vitamin or herbal formula. So we've tried to make the science a little more digestible.

Hyaluronic acid is a gel that is found in soft tissue throughout your body. Its function is to lubricate and cushion tissue whether that tissue is part of your skin, joints, eyes, cartilage, blood vessels, heart valves, whatever. It accomplishes that function in a couple of ways:

- HA is a major component of your extracellular matrix (the liquid between your cells). There, HA retains water, hydrates your cells, and provides a medium to carry nutrients to cells and waste away from them. In short, it keeps your cells healthy and resilient.
- HA is also a primary constituent of synovial fluid (the liquid that fills each joint cavity). There, it serves as a shock-absorber for your knees, ankles, elbows, etc. HA also serves as the primary source of nutrients for your cartilage. (Cartilage isn't connected to the blood system, consequently it can't get nutrients from the blood stream.)
- HA supports the formation and maintenance of collagen. As the principal protein in human skin, bone, cartilage, tendons, and connective tissue, healthy collagen levels are critical to

skin, joint, and bone health.

- Finally, HA contains glucosamine—a carbohydrate that supports joint health and has become an effective supplement for many osteoarthritis sufferers. (In fact, it's so common you can probably find it right next to the aspirin in your grocery store.)

HA's impact on your skin is obvious, keeping it smooth and moisturized. It also helps your skin resist and repair bruises and cuts by helping cells move to new tissue sites. In less obvious ways, HA provides exactly the same benefit to joints, eyes, and other parts of your body.

As we age, however, our bodies produce less HA. Production starts to lag around age 20. By 40, diminished supplies of HA leave us with those aches, pains, and wrinkles we've always thought were "unavoidable parts of aging." So all we have to do is supplement our HA levels, right? Unlike many of the natural remedies you've read about here, it just wasn't that easy with HA. But today it's possible, thanks to some new advances.

HA supplements: Two decades in the making thanks to two big challenges

Mainstream medicine began studying and using hyaluronic acid 20 years ago. It developed a few products to heal wounds, burns, sores, and surgical incisions, to speed recovery from eye surgery, and to ease the symptoms of advanced osteoarthritis. But researchers ran into two problems when they started developing HA treatments. First, it doesn't last long in the body (so you have to take it frequently). Second, in their natural state, HA molecules are so large that they can't pass through the intestinal tract and into the blood stream. In other words, raw HA cannot be effective when taken orally.

Consequently, HA hasn't yielded many convenient treatment options. Osteoarthritis sufferers, for example, have gotten substantial relief from HA treatment. (HA provided better pain relief than naproxen in one study.[1]) However, the regimen involves getting injections in the joint (usually the knee) five times a week. Not surprisingly, the pain and inflammation caused by the treatment was sometimes as severe as the pain and inflammation caused by the disease!

Mini molecules offer big benefits

Alternative medicine researchers, however, claim they can now access the benefits of hyaluronic acid through a dietary supplement. Deanne Dolnick, an educator with Soft Gel Technologies in California, says researchers have found a way to reduce the size of HA molecules so that they can pass through the lining of the digestive system and deliver potent HA to the blood stream.

"There are scientists in Japan who have patented an enzyme-cleaving technique," Dolnick says. "What they have done is they have made hyaluronic acid into smaller polymers so that it's a smaller version of the original without chemically altering it. It functions in the body just as hyaluronic acid would." Right now, the evidence showing that HA can be effective as an oral supplement is limited. But some does exist.

Wounds heal 5 days faster

In one test, researchers anesthetized lab rats and gave them each identical skin wounds. The animals were divided into three groups: One group received 3,000 mg/kg of oral HA daily (in the form of Injuv™ supplements), the second group received an oral placebo daily, the third group received daily topical doses of a commercial wound-healing ointment. Researchers measured the wounds each day for ten days and concluded that oral HA dramatically reduced healing time. Rats fed HA healed within 13 days—five days faster than placebo-fed rats. In addition, the HA delivered almost as much benefit as the commercial wound-healing ointment. Rats treated with the ointment took 10.6 days to heal.[2]

Over 80 percent of study participants report "great improvement"

Healing wounds on rats was a promising start. But researchers still needed to determine if HA could improve the skin of creatures that aren't covered in fur. So researchers at Ohtsuma University in Japan conducted a small trial with humans. They monitored the impact of oral HA on 96 women, aged 22 to 65. Every day for 45 days, the subjects consumed six capsules of Injuv. Each capsule contained 6.3 mg of hyaluronic acid, for a total daily dose of 37.8 mg. More than 80 percent of the women reported "great improvement" in skin moisture, smoothness, and firmness on their faces, hands, elbows, knees, and heels. More than 70 percent noticed significant relief from stiff shoulders and joints.

According to Dolnick, hyaluronic acid has not triggered any adverse side effects in people using Soft Gel's HA supplement. (Extracted from roosters' combs, the product could theoretically trigger allergic reactions in people sensitive to chicken or eggs. But so far, none have been reported.) The product has also passed an oral toxicity study in which 10 rats (five male and five female) were given 5050 mg/kg daily for four days. The high dose triggered diarrhea in some animals, but no other side effects. Researchers found no abnormalities when they later euthanized and autopsied the animals.[3]

Wrinkle reduction in a lemon-flavored drink

Obviously, some results posted from skin care studies are inevitably subjective. When it comes to determining how dry a person's skin feels, researchers often must rely on the impressions of the test subjects. But researchers can measure changes in wrinkles and other visible skin conditions. Lane Labs, conducted a small scale human trial of Toki—that all-natural secret of Japan's porcelain-skinned beauties—and obtained some impressive results.

Toki is a different kind of supplement. Sold in powder form, Toki is mixed with cold water to create a drink that tastes like generously sweetened lemonade, and contains several ingredients that can promote skin and joint health—hyaluronic acid, collagen, calcium, vitamin C, glucosamine, and seaweed extract.

Iron out wrinkles in as little as two weeks

Researchers asked 38 women ages 35 to 65 to take Toki for eight weeks (three times a day for the first two weeks to achieve a "loading dose," then twice a day for the remaining six weeks). Each woman's face was examined and photographed at the beginning of the study, focusing particularly on wrinkles, puffiness, and sagging around the eyes. Researchers re-examined each woman every two weeks for the duration of the study. They documented significant reduction of wrinkles and other signs of facial aging after just two weeks of supplementation, and dramatic improvement by the end of the study. Through a series of blood tests, they also determined that participants' blood collagen levels actually increased an average of 114 percent after 30 days of supplementing with Toki.

One-third of the women experienced mild to moderate side effects from the treatment (primarily itching and gastrointestinal upset). However, those conditions disappeared quickly and did not prompt any women to discontinue the supplement. After all, remember, women are injecting poison into their faces to get similar results. So what's a little gas or scratching?

Laugh lines might not be all you lose…

The women in Lane Labs' study also reported one unexpected effect. They lost weight. On average, each participant lost two pounds during the study, although some women dropped as much as seven pounds. "We're not promoting it as a weight-loss product," says Jennifer Nissen, N.D., Lane Labs' manager of nutritional research. She suspects Toki's collagen content was responsible for the incidental weight loss. "Collagen is a protein and protein helps level out your blood sugar, decreasing blood sugar crashes and sugar cravings. Protein is also filling, so if women drink it before a meal, they may eat less."

Beauty…at a price

Regardless of whether it's new and alternative, Toki holds true to one old adage: Beauty doesn't come cheap. A box containing 60 packets of Toki sells for $195 plus shipping. That means younger skin is going to cost you roughly $200 a month (and closer to $300 in the first month when the recommended dosage is higher). But then again, Botox treatments start at about $300 per injection. And a small bottle (1.7 ounces) of Clinique's "anti-aging serum" will set you back more than $50. Any way you look at it, the fountain of youth comes with a steep price tag.

If you want to try HA but don't want to have to sell the farm, there's an alternative. Straight hyaluronic acid supplements are cheaper than Toki. A month's supply of Injuv (which is currently being marketed under the brand name SkinGlow) costs $62.50. See below to find out how to order either of these products.

Member Source Directory

Osteophase, Tango Advanced Nutrition; tel. (866)778-2646 or (805)845-5011; www.puretango.com. Special HSI-member pricing: A 30-capsule bottle costs US$26.95 plus shipping. A 60-capsule bottle costs US$45.95 plus shipping.

SkinGlow, Nuricology; tel. (800)545-9960 or (510)263-2000; website www.nutricology.com. A bottle of 150 softgels is US$62.50 plus shipping.

Toki, Compassionet, P.O. Box 710, Saddle River, NJ 07458; tel. (800)510-2010; fax (201)236-0090; www.compassionet.com. US$149.95 plus s/h.

References

Replenish your body's supply of this natural moisturizer and say goodbye to wrinkles and joint pain
1 *The Journal of Rheumatology*, 1998; (25)11: p. 2,203-12
2 Research report of MDS Panlabs Pharmacology Services, Taiwan
3 Quality assurance report from StillMeadow Inc., March 2000

THE PERFECT PROSTATE CURE: TODAY'S ...

CANCER

Report 7

The Perfect Prostate Cure:
Today's Greatest Medicines for Men

THE PERFECT PROSTATE CURE: TODAY'S MEDICINES FOR MEN

Contents

Chapter 1

Vietnamese medicinal herb shows promise in healing prostate and ovarian disease

We talk a lot about traditional Chinese medicine and the inroads it's made as a modern approach to healing. But we never focused much on traditional Vietnamese medicine until we learned about one of its most valuable herbs called crinum latifolium. Apparently, it's so revered in Vietnam that it used to be reserved only for royalty and was known both as the "Medicine for the King's Palace" and the "Royal Female Herb."

Those traditional references actually highlight one of crinum's most unique aspects—its ability to target both prostate and ovarian health concerns. But crinum seems to be an equal opportunity herb. And its benefits seem to go beyond just sex-specific diseases too.

First, let's talk about what it can do to protect you from prostate or ovarian diseases.

Picking up where PC Spes left off— without the risk

Although most of the research on crinum focuses on men, it all started when the Hoang family studied its effect on ovarian health.

Dr. Kha Hoang was the Chief Teacher and medical doctor for the Vietnamese royal family. In 1984 his daughter had so many cysts on her ovary that surgery was planned to remove it. Dr. Hoang had her start drinking a tea made with crinum leaves, and about six weeks later the cysts were gone.

Today, three generations of the Hoang family are integrated medicine practitioners. The family has used crinum together with other supportive herbs in treating a variety of prostate and ovarian conditions. Biopsies confirmed 16 cases of advanced prostate cancer were completely cured regardless of prostate specific antigen (PSA) levels. In fact, sometimes PSA levels go up in men taking crinum, even though testing shows that their prostate cells are normal and healthy. That is exactly what happened to Ken Malik, the co-founder and Executive Director of the Prostate Awareness Foundation, a non-profit organization based in San Francisco, California.

In his own battle with prostate cancer, Malik chose to take the natural approach—opting for a therapeutic regimen of nutrition and exercise. He also used the herbal supplement PC Spes for eight years and found doing so stabilized his condition. PC Spes was marketed as an herbal formula that had shown remarkable results in treating prostate problems. Recently though, it was pulled from the market after researchers discovered that some PC Spes products claiming to be all-natural actually contained synthetic, potentially harmful substances. Malik was one of millions of men worldwide affected when PC Spes was taken off the market. When he stopped taking it, his PSA level started to creep upward. So he began his search for a replacement. That led him to crinum.

He started taking it in January 2002, and, over the course of the next 10 months, his PSA actually continued to go up. Most of the time, this would be cause for concern. But Malik's most recent biopsy showed only healthy tissue. His experience might add some support to recent reports that claim the PSA test might not be the best indicator of prostate cancer risk.

Malik was excited enough about his own experience to organize an informal trial with 10 members of the Prostate Awareness Foundation. Participants were told to take nine crinum tablets each day for three months. All 10 noted some kind of functional improvement.

Not everyone using crinum experiences elevated PSA levels. Sometimes its benefits follow a more predictable path, like the testimonial the manufacturer shared with me from a 58-year-old man who had a PSA of 93 when he went to his urologist for treatment. He'd waited so long that his cancer had spread to his bones, intestines, and lymph nodes. He was placed on an aggressive herbal program that included crinum. After just four months, his PSA was down to .9 and the symptoms he'd been experiencing—difficulty urinating, swelling in his legs, and extreme fatigue—had all disappeared.

92.6 percent success for BPH symptoms

Crinum isn't just for prostate cancer or extremely advanced cases of prostate disease. It also appears to alleviate the symptoms of one of the most common male problems—enlarged prostate, or benign prostatic hyperplasia (BPH). The main symptom of BPH is frequent and sometimes painful urination. There are over 500 individual case histories of successful crinum treatment for BPH. And after seven years of research, the International Hospital in Vietnam reported that 92.6 percent of patients had good results using crinum for BPH (confirmed by measurements of prostate size and clinical evaluation by urologists).[1] However, these results have not been confirmed in Western studies.

Helping your cells communicate

As effective as crinum appears to be, there's still no official consensus as to why or how it works. Researchers think it may have something to do with how it affects you at the simplest level—the cellular level. The human body contains about 70 trillion cells. With a few exceptions, each of these individual cells is a living entity with its own complete set of genes. Each of these cells maintains its own existence and also makes a vital contribution to your life and health. But in order for your body to function properly, all of those cells must communicate. For instance, your muscles must contract only when your brain sends a message to contract and not any other time.

Cells also communicate with one another to determine the correct balance of cell proliferation and apoptosis, or death. Basically, they're constantly working together to regulate how many cells you have—and how healthy they are—at any given moment. But if your cells aren't communicating properly, apoptosis may not happen the way it should, which means that unhealthy, even cancerous, cells can continue to thrive and mutate. Recent experiments show that crinum extract helps cells produce a substance called neopterin, which they send out to communicate with immune cells, calling them into action against cancer and other foreign invaders.[2]

Five more ways to knock out disease

I found a crinum supplement called Healthy Prostate & Ovary that also contains five other herbal ingredients—alisima plantago-quatica, astragalus, momordica charantia, carica papaya leaf, and annona muricata leaf—all known for their immune- and energy-boosting effects as well as their abilities to regulate abnormal body functions.

Crinum is so established and widely used as a treatment for prostate and ovary diseases in Vietnam that their crops of the herb are generally prohibited from being exported. So Healthy Prostate & Ovary is one of the first crinum products we know of to be made available in the U.S. See the Member Source Directory on page 71 for complete ordering information.

If you decide to try the Healthy Prostate & Ovary formula, the recommended dose is three 600-mg tablets three times daily. And, as always, if you're battling cancer or any other serious illness, please consult with your physician before using this or any other product.

Chapter 2

How you can take advantage of the AMAS Cancer Test

The AMAS Cancer Test stands for Anti-Malignan Antibody in Serum test. Malignin is a peptide found in people with a wide range of cancers. If the anti-malignan antibody is detected in the blood, it means that the body detected the presence of this peptide, and launched an immune response against it. Clinical studies have shown that the AMAS test is up to 95 percent accurate on the first reading, and up to 99 percent accurate after two readings.

In one study at Beth Israel Hospital in New York, the AMAS test demonstrated amazing accuracy. Within the study group of 125 people, the test was positive for 21 people who were later confirmed to have cancer, while it was negative for 97 people who showed no signs of cancer. The remaining seven people produced positive readings on the AMAS test but showed no signs of cancer; yet the study notes that all were symptomatic, had a family history of cancer, or both—indicating that the AMAS test may have detected a problem that conventional screening methods could not find.

This simple blood test can detect precancerous and cancerous cells with up to 99 percent sensitivity. Many of our members wrote in to say they were having difficulty finding a doctor willing to do the test—because they had never heard of it.

At HSI, we're committed to bringing you breakthrough information on the latest health discoveries. Our research often brings information directly to you before it even reaches your doctor. We realize there's no benefit to providing you with cutting-edge information if you can't use it. So our team did some research to learn more about the availability of the AMAS test and how you can take advantage of it.

Luckily, we were able to speak directly with Dr. Samuel Bogoch, one of the two doctors who first discovered the anti-malignin antibody and developed the AMAS test. He said that the test has been available for some time, but so far, doctors have only learned of it through word of mouth. Recent efforts have started getting the word out—but there is a still a long way to go.

You don't need a doctor's permission to order the AMAS test

But the good news is that ANYONE can order an AMAS test. Just call 1-800-922-8378 and leave your name and address to receive a free kit in the mail. The kit includes the materials and instructions you need to complete the test, and a packet of scientific literature supporting its benefits. Then, take the kit to your doctor, and ask him to order a blood sample and sign the analysis form. All AMAS tests are analyzed by Dr. Bogoch's staff in Boston (overnight shipping instructions are included in the kit). As some members have found, some labs refuse to draw specimens for tests that will be performed at another lab. According to Dr. Bogoch, that's more often the case

with smaller labs; larger labs usually send specimens to other labs on a daily basis. If your doctor's lab is not willing to process the AMAS test, and your doctor is not willing to find one that will, do some research on your own. Check the Yellow Pages and call around to larger labs in your area.

Some readers also asked about the availability of the AMAS test outside the U.S. Anyone from anywhere in the world can order the test. The only unique challenge is the shipping. Samples sent from outside the U.S. may need to ship in dry ice to ensure a valid sample. The analysis costs $135 (not including extra lab fees or shipping costs), but the test is Medicare approved; and remember, ordering the kit is completely free.

The AMAS test can detect the presence of cancerous cells, but can't pinpoint their location. So a positive reading must be followed up by additional testing to locate the cancer and determine its stage. But the test does come much closer to offering true early detection than many other screening methods, and does so in a non-invasive way. To learn even more about AMAS, you can visit this website: www.amascancertest.com.

If you're interested in the AMAS test, you don't have to wait for your doctor to hear about it. Call and order the free kit, and review the research. If you're still interested, take the kit and the literature to your doctor.

Member Source Directory

Healthy Prostate & Ovary; Nutricology; tel. (800)545-9960 or (510)263-2000; www.nutricology.com. A 180-tablet bottle costs US$50.00 plus shipping. HSI members receive a 20% discount on the purchase of two bottles.

AMAS Cancer Test, tel. (800)922-8378; www.amascancertest.com.

References

Vietnamese medicinal herb shows promise in healing prostate and ovarian disease
1 Zvetkova E, Wirleitner B, Tram NT, Schennach H, Fuchs D Aqueous extracts of Crinum latifolium (L.) and Camellia sinensis show immunomodulatory properties in human peripheral blood mononuclear cells. *Int Immunopharmacol.* 2001 Nov;1(12):2143-50

Diabetes Defeated:

From Insulin Dependent to Non-Diabetic in 6 Weeks Flat

DIABETES DEFEATED: FROM INSULIN DEPENDENT TO NON-DIABETIC IN 6 WEEKS FLAT

Contents

Chapter 1

Prevent—even reverse—diabetes damage with the vitamin "teacher" breakthrough

Think of glucose as a school yard bully constantly goading your cells and getting them into trouble. If you're a diabetic, all of your cells are surrounded by blood that contains elevated glucose levels. Many of them manage to remain unaffected and keep internal glucose levels normal. But certain cells are unable to regulate glucose and instead develop high internal levels of sugar, which they can't completely metabolize. This creates reactive oxidative stress (ROS) within the cell and sends your body into a tailspin that can result in conditions typically associated with diabetes, such as neuropathy and vision loss.[1] And once these conditions set in, they're usually permanent, since there are no mainstream drugs or other formulas designed specifically to treat the complications of diabetes.

So your cells need help in order to learn how to exist in the negative environment associated with high blood sugar. What they need is a positive role model. And research is now showing that the simple B-vitamin thiamine might be just the teacher your cells need.

We've found a new form of thiamine that has only recently become available in the United States. Just a small amount prevents glucose-induced problems from occurring and may also help reverse damage that's already been done.

Are you "browning" with AGE?

It's a vitamin we don't hear much about, but, in fact, your body needs thiamine more than you might imagine—especially if you're a diabetic. It plays a vital role in carbohydrate metabolism within all cells of the human body. There have been suggestions for many years that diabetic patients have impaired absorption of thiamine and may display low levels of thiamine deficiency.[2] Plus, surges of glucose can destroy thiamine, leaving the cells with a functional deficiency, meaning they still work but not as well as they could if they had the thiamine they need. If your thiamine level is deficient, it throws the whole system off. Without adequate thiamine, your cells are literally soaking in a toxic glucose bath. This gives glucose ample opportunity to move in and cause all sorts of problems, from fatigue to neuropathy.

High plasma glucose concentrations are responsible for increased mitochondrial free radical production and subsequent inactivation of your cells' natural protectors. To add to the problem, not only are your cells' natural defense mechanisms disabled, but glucose also activates three pathways of metabolic damage and boosts the formation of advanced glycation endproducts, or AGEs, as they're appropriately called. AGEs are the end result of the complex chemical process through which the structure of proteins is warped by exposure to sugars or by other, much more reactive molecules. AGE chemistry is the cause of the "browning" you see when you roast a chicken or make toast, but the same process is at work in your body every day of your life—in your arteries, your kidneys, your heart, your eyes, your skin, your nerves. In every cell, the sugar that your body uses for fuel is busily at work at this very moment, browning your body and leading to problems like fatigue and premature aging.

Essentially, glucose harmfully saturates your cells and destroys their natural defense mechanisms. But by normalizing thiamine levels in the cells, you can help your cells learn how to navigate this environment by activating alternative paths and offsetting negative reactions like the formation of AGEs. As a result, metabolic balance may be restored, potentially protecting against kidney, eye, and nerve damage due to diabetes.[4]

Knowing all this, researchers tested the potential benefits of supplementing with thiamine, but all the available thiamine supplements were water soluble, and the body breaks them down and excretes them too quickly for any therapeutic effect to set in. So, thanks to problems with absorption, initial thiamine/diabetes research exhibited less-than-impressive results. But more recently, researchers released a study using a fat/lipid-soluble form of thiamine. This study not only confirmed scientists' original hypotheses about thiamine's potential for diabetes but also confirmed hope for millions of people looking for ways to fight back against the disease.

300% boost in enzyme activity holds off damage from diabetes

The factor that made the significant difference in this study is a supplement called benfotiamine, a lipid/fat soluble derivative of vitamin B1 (thiamine). In the presence of allicin, the active principle of garlic, the water-soluble thiamine hydrochloride is transformed into a lipid-soluble compound.[5] According to studies, as an oral supplement, benfotiamine is absorbed more rapidly and for longer periods than water-soluble thiamine.[6-10] And its unique structure enabled it to pass directly through cell membranes, readily crossing the intestinal wall and being taken straight to the cell. As a result, your body absorbs benfotiamine better than thiamine itself and levels of thiamine remain higher for longer. Thiamine absorption from benfotiamine is about five times higher than conventional thiamine supplements. So benfotiamine has more time and opportunity to work with your cells, teaching them how to handle the difficult situations glucose puts them in.

Benfotiamine was developed in Japan in the late 1950s to treat alcoholic neuropathy, sciatica, and other painful nerve conditions. Japanese researchers patented the process in1962. It has been used for over a decade in Germany. And although it has been used successfully for over 12 years in Europe for the prevention and relief of symptoms in people already suffering with various neuropathies, it has only recently been introduced into the United States.[11]

Benfotiamine came into the American limelight when a research team led by Dr. Michael Brownlee published the results of its study. Initially, the researchers set out to inhibit or block damage to the cells by using thiamine to boost the activity of a substance called transketolase, which provides a way for the cells to use up the glucose metabolites that are responsible for most of the damage seen in diabetes.[12]

Transketolase does this by safely directing excess glucose to the correct pathway, offsetting potential cellular damage. However, standard thiamine only increased transketolase activity by about 20 percent.

German research colleagues suggested the lipid-soluble thiamine that had been used for over a decade in Germany—benfotiamine. According to Dr. Brownlee, the results were dramatically better:

"It turned out that benfotiamine boosted the activity of the enzyme transketolase by 300 to 400 percent—something we never could have predicted."

The end result of increased transketolase is reduced levels of glucose. But benfotiamine may take this one step further. By boosting transketolase's activity, the researchers reasoned, benfotiamine might be able to reverse glucose's reckless activity—essentially converting the two damage-triggering glucose metabolites into harmless chemicals and preventing all three damaging biochemical pathways from being activated.

Small drop in glucose levels has a major impact on symptoms

HSI often talks alot about how small changes in things like exercise and diet can make a big difference for diabetics. To demonstrate how significant even a small reduction of glucose can be, consider the Diabetes Control and Complications Trail, which was conducted from 1983 to 1993 by the National Institute of Diabetes and Digestive and Kidney Diseases (NIDDK). This study showed that keeping blood glucose levels as close to normal as possible slows the onset and progression of eye, kidney, and nerve diseases caused by diabetes.

In fact, it demonstrated that any sustained lowering of blood glucose helps—even if the person has a history of poor control. HbA1c (glycosylated hemoglobin) reflects average blood glucose levels over a two- or three-month period. In this study, researchers found that even a 2 percent decrease of blood glucose levels was associated with dramatic results: a 75 percent reduction in risk of developing eye disease, a 50 percent reduction in the risk of kidney disease, and a 60 percent reduction in nerve disease.[13]

Dr. Brownlee's animal research with benfotiamine supports these findings. His chemical analysis showed that all three potential damage-causing biochemical pathways had been "normalized" in the benfotiamine-treated diabetic laboratory animals so that their retinas were biochemically identical to normal retinas. Benfotiamine also prevented diabetic retinopathy in the animals, since microscopic examination revealed that the retinas of benfotiamine-treated diabetic animals were free of vascular damage.

Numerous other researchers have concentrated their efforts on benfotiamine's AGE-blocking mechanisms because they would limit the wear and tear on the body's cells and allow individuals, particularly diabetics, to live longer and healthier lives. In the research we've seen, benfotiamine has emerged as the premier AGE inhibitor.[14-20]

Dosage concerns require extra care

Dr. Brownlee is currently applying to the U.S. Food and Drug Administration to test benfotiamine as an Investigational New Drug. Since his research has been focused on animals, he is eager to study benfotiamine's potential human benefits.

Although some dosage regimens start out with high doses and scale back down, Robert C. Holladay, M.S., who has compiled a great deal of benfotiamine research, recommends a more moderate approach. He asserts that, "Ingestion of benfotiamine may result in the elimination of AGE-protein cross-links, which are a major constituent of arterial plaque. I am concerned about the rapid manner in which it may cause the removal of plaque from blood vessels. If the plaque is being removed, a large chunk might break off and cause a stroke or heart attack. If I was older than 60 or if I had a serious problem with high blood pressure I would probably start out by taking very low doses of benfotiamine and gradually increase my dosage. Of course, there are no reports of strokes or heart attacks from benfotiamine in the medical literature, but it is a thought to consider."[21]

Many researchers suggest beginning with a lower daily dose and then raising the amount every two weeks until benefits are being realized. This approach would look something like this: 200 to 300 mg per day for the first two weeks, then raise the dose to 300 to 450 mg daily. You may need to increase your dosage to 400 to 600 mg daily, depending on the severity of your condition. Once you reach the ideal level for you, this becomes your maintenance dose.

Benfotiamine, combined with exercise and a balanced diet, appears to be the next step in fighting diabetes and preventing it from causing too much damage to cells. Or as I like to think of it, a way for you and your cells to really teach glucose who's boss.

Chapter 2

Dodge the sugar bullet—and double your chances of beating this leading killer

For years, HSI Panelist Jon Barron had resisted suggestions that he devise an approach for battling diabetes. His reluctance, he told me, stemmed from his belief that using formulas to manage the symptoms of diabetes without dealing with the underlying causes ultimately fails. The responsible approach, he thought, was to help people optimize the health of the organs in the body that control blood sugar levels—not to treat the symptoms after people had the disease.

But the realities of the American diet finally changed his mind, and he began to look at botanicals that could actually accomplish both things simultaneously, help control blood sugar levels and help rebuild the organs that control those levels— not just in diabetics and pre-diabetics, but in anyone eating a less than perfect diet.

A number of herbs, including milk thistle, bitter melon, ginseng, and aloe, are used to control blood sugar. Ayurvedic medicine offers more than 44 different herbal therapies and formulas for diabetes. Both fenugreek and gymnema, for example, come from this tradition. And these two have been the subject of 30 different studies of varying degrees of scientific rigor in Indian and Western literature. Only two did not favor the treatment being tested.

After investigating a number of botanicals, Barron settled on four. The first two come from the Ayurvedic tradition and the third from Japan. There is extensive research, including clinical trials, on these three. The fourth, nopal cactus, has a folk tradition in the American Southwest and Mexico; research on it is promising, but not as extensive as the others.

It's worth noting that several of these botanicals also impact high blood pressure and abnormal blood lipid levels, both characteristics of pre-diabetes, as well as blood sugar levels. Evidence suggests that one even regenerates cells in the pancreas, which, in turn, facilitates healthier insulin levels.

Blood sugar levels plummet by 30 percent with one herb

Seeds from fenugreek plants (*Trigonella foenum-gracum*) have long been used in India, Africa, and the Middle East to treat gastrointestinal problems, gout, wounds, hyperlipidemia, and diabetes. Clinical research dating back to 1939 suggests that fenugreek helps normalize how the body absorbs and uses glucose. The seeds contain a rare type of fiber that forms a gel inside the stomach, reducing its ability to absorb sugar and fat. The gel also makes the stomach feel full faster and longer, promoting weight loss.

On average, participants in fenugreek clinical trials have seen their fasting blood sugar drop by 30 percent, their sugar levels after eating drop 20 to 35 percent, and their hemoglobin A1C drop by 12 percent. (The A1C test is an index of diabetes severity that measures the average amount of sugar molecules that have attached to red blood cells.) In one study, participants experienced a 54 percent drop in urinary glucose levels.[1]

Other clinical trials have shown that fenugreek can reduce total cholesterol, LDL and triglyceride levels, particularly in individuals suffering from coronary artery disease and type 2 diabetes.[2,3] In short, it may help diabetics reduce both their blood sugar and blood lipid levels.

However, the news isn't all good. To get those effects, some study participants had to take large amounts-as much as 100 grams a day-of a herb that tastes acutely bitter and makes for foul smelling sweat and urine. In addition, fenugreek can trigger some side effects, specifically cramping, diarrhea, flatulence and other gastrointestinal disorders. But a recently developed extract eliminates some side effects (specifically, the taste and odor) and concentrates the active ingredient, making smaller doses possible. Fenugreek, however, is still contraindicated in some circumstances. Because of its high fiber content, it can alter your absorption of other medications (such as anticoagulants, MAO inhibitors, and hypoglycemic medications) and change their effectiveness.

Herbal "sugar killer" makes sweets hit a sour note

A woody vine used in Indian medicine for over 2,000 years, gymnema sylvestre is commonly known as the "sugar destroyer." A peptide found in the plant blocks certain receptor sites on our taste buds and eventually makes sugar taste, well, not sweet.[4] But gymnema does more to ease diabetes symptoms than quell our sugar cravings.

Gymnemic acid (a key active ingredient) fills sugar receptor sites in the intestine, too, making them unavailable to ingested sugars. If the sugar you eat

doesn't get digested, it doesn't filter into your bloodstream. Clinical research also indicates that gymnema regenerates beta cells in the pancreas (which are involved in insulin production), stimulates the release of increased amounts of insulin, and increases the permeability of cells so that they absorb more insulin.[5]

Several clinical studies have measured gymnema's effect on both type 1 and type 2 diabetes. Type 1 diabetics who took 400 mg for 6 to 30 months saw their blood sugar levels drop 52.6 percent on average.[6] Most participants in an 18-month study achieved such significant and consistent blood sugar decreases that they were able to reduce their medication. Five participants were able to discontinue insulin use entirely and maintain healthy blood sugar levels by taking only 400 mg of gymnema sylvestre extract daily.[7]

To date, no one has reported experiencing adverse side effects from the herb, and it is not contraindicated for any condition. No tests, however, have been conducted to determine whether it can be safely taken by pregnant women.

Ancient blood sugar controlling secret also drops blood pressure and cholesterol

You've probably never heard of konjac mannan (I know I hadn't before I started researching this article), but it's been used as a food remedy for over 1,000 years in Japan. And it's also been tested in a number of clinical trials. In a 65-day trial, 72 patients with adult-onset diabetes who took konjac saw their fasting blood sugar levels drop an average of 51.8 percent and their levels after eating drop 84.6 percent.[8] In an eight-week trial, pre-diabetics reported improvements in their blood sugar and cholesterol levels. On average, their total cholesterol dropped by 12.4 percent, LDL levels dropped by 22 percent, and LDL/HDL ratios fell by 22.2 percent.[9]

Other benefits have been reported for konjac. Patients with type 2 diabetes also suffering from high cholesterol and high blood pressure experienced an average drop in their systolic blood pressure of 6.9 percent after supplementing with konjac mannan.[10] Twenty obese individuals who took konjac for eight weeks lost an average of 5.5 pounds even though they were explicitly told not to change their diet or exercise routines. They also experienced significant reductions in their LDL and total cholesterol levels.[11]

At the University of Toronto, researchers concluded that konjac mannan extract is two to four times more effective than pectin, psyllium, guar, oats, and other fibers at reducing cholesterol. It also proved to be equally effective as statin drugs at lowering LDL cholesterol and as some conventional diabetic agents, such as Acarbose, at controlling blood sugar levels.[12]

Fiber-rich Indian remedy solves prickly problem of sugar/fat conversion

Leaves from the nopal cactus, commonly known as the prickly pear cactus, have long been regarded as health food by native peoples in Mexico and southwestern United States. There's not a lot of clinical research into the botanical's medicinal benefits, but anecdotal evidence and several small studies suggest that eating nopal leaves with a meal can help contain and even reduce serum glucose levels.[13] Individuals with type 2 diabetes have experienced a 10 to 20 percent reduction in blood sugar levels after eating nopal. Researchers aren't certain how nopal lowers blood sugar, but they suggest that its rich fiber content inhibits the absorption of glucose in the intestinal tract.

A larger body of research indicates that nopal can reduce both cholesterol and triglyceride levels.[14] Researchers have suggested that it accomplishes this by eliminating excess bile acids (which eventually turn into cholesterol) and by inhibiting the conversion of blood sugar into fat.

This four-in-one solution kicks sugar and fat metabolism into overdrive

These four botanicals make up what Jon Barron refers to as his "sugar, lipid metabolic enhancement formula," officially called Glucotor. It's designed to offset the impact of high-sugar, high-fat foods. In pre-diabetics and non-diabetics, it can help promote healthier blood sugar and cholesterol levels...and a healthier weight. Jon told me he takes it himself on occasion and avoids the sleepiness that follows a few hours after indulging in a meal that's a little too rich or too sweet.

For diabetics, Glucotor may have even bigger ramifications. Although the formula hasn't undergone clinical trials, one physician has tested it in his family practice in Evansville, Indiana, on diabetic patients. According to Barron, "It produced results that the doctors have not seen before, even with hard core drugs," including dramatic changes in blood sugar levels.

Patients find fast diabetes and hypertension relief—without prescription drugs

To find out more, I called Anthony Hall, M.D., the physician in Indiana. It turns out that he's in training to be a naturopathic doctor, and he was happy to provide information on the 15 patients who agreed to take the formula.

Three of them, he told me, dropped out of the trial due to digestive problems caused by the product. (The formula can stimulate large, urgent bowel movements, so people just starting the supplement may want to take only half of the standard daily dose and give their digestive systems a chance to adjust.)

He monitored the effect of Glucotor on his patients' blood sugar, blood pressure, and cholesterol levels, and cautions that, if you're on medication to control any of those levels, you absolutely should consult with your doctor before trying Glucotor and arrange to have your levels checked regularly.

One of Dr. Hall's patients was a 56-year-old woman who had been on varying doses of insulin and oral hypoglycemics since she was diagnosed with diabetes in 1993. Before she began taking Glucotor, her hemoglobin A1C level was 9.0. (A reading of 9 indicates severe diabetes, while 6 or less indicates a healthy, non-diabetic condition.) Over the course of taking Glucotor for six weeks, she discontinued her insulin and Metformin (the generic form of Glucophage, one of the most common prescription drugs used to treat diabetes) and reduced her oral hypoglycemic from 8 mg to 2 mg per day. At the end of the trial, a second test showed her A1C level had fallen to 5.7, a healthy, non-diabetic level.

During our conversation, Dr. Hall also told me how surprised he was to see dramatic changes in blood lipid levels in some of his Glucotor patients. One man's total cholesterol dropped from 297 to 210 and his triglycerides from 580 to 506 after four weeks of taking the supplement. Another patient, a woman this time, had a 23.5 percent reduction in her total cholesterol, a 32 percent drop in her LDL level, and an 18 percent drop in her triglycerides. After 5.5 weeks of taking Glucotor, her blood pressure dropped from 140/96 to around 115/75, and she was able to discontinue taking Lipitor and her blood pressure medication.

And these are just a few examples of the great responses Dr. Hall saw in his patients. Since then, the formula has racked up an impressive 82 percent success rate. Most people would look at those results and be satisfied. But Barron wasn't. So he decided to reformulate Glucotor.

The result is a new and improved version of Glucotor (Glucotor v.2), which includes an all-natural ingredient that has been proven to boost the body's insulin response 20-fold. This one addition to the original formula has made the already miraculous Glucotor up to 300 percent more effective than similar products without the potential of toxic side effects.

Make your insulin receptors more receptive

But why reformulate at all when you've already got something with such a high success rate you literally can't keep it on the shelves? Simply put, Barron says the success rate just wasn't high enough considering it's a human statistic. He couldn't see past the 18 percent of people that he wasn't helping.

That led him on a search for other ingredients he could add to boost Glucotor's effectiveness. And once again, he arrived back at cinnamon. But this time he found a specific cinnamon extract, called Cinnulin PF, which eliminated the roadblocks he'd encountered before.

So just what is Cinnulin PF? Well, as Barron puts it, "it's pretty amazing. It's a patented cinnamon extract that operates at the cellular and molecular levels. It actually works to make the insulin receptor sites on your individual body cells more receptive. If you have enough cinnamon every day, you can actually increase your body's insulin response threefold. That's 300 percent—and that's a big deal."

I wanted to find out more about Cinnulin PF so I went straight to the source: Integrity Nutraceuticals Inter-national (INI). INI is a raw material supplier of bulk nutraceuticals including amino acids, herbs, and specialty compounds like Cinnulin PF.

All the benefit, none of the risks

Until recently methylhydroxy-chalcone polymer (or MHCP) was thought to be the active compound in cinnamon responsible for the beneficial effect on blood glucose. It turns out that early research misidentified the substances responsible for these actions as cinnamon's MHCP fractions. The substances actually providing the blood-sugar-lowering benefits are water-soluble polyphenol polymers called Type-A polymers.[15]

INI created an aqueous cinnamon extract product using a process that removes the potentially harmful compounds from whole cinnamon while leaving the Type-A polymers intact (using no chemical solvents). Extracts made with solvents other than water will actually extract the lipid-soluble portion of cinnamon, which contains the potentially harmful fractions.

Actually, this process makes Cinnulin PF even stronger than it would be without it: The lipid soluble portion of cinnamon has been shown to have no effect on glucose metabolism. But in contrast, the water-soluble portion has been proven to increase glucose uptake by 20-fold.[16]

Early research looks promising

In diabetes, either the body doesn't produce enough insulin or the cells resist it, so the sugar remains in the blood, builds up to higher and higher levels, and ultimately starts damaging protein-based tissue and organs. Cinnulin PF triggers receptor sensitivity to insulin and primes the receptor for glucose uptake.

In one study, researchers tested cinnamon's effects by using a water-based cinnamon extract similar to Cinnulin PF on 28 people with Type II diabetes. Patients received 500 mg of a formula containing water extracts of cinnamon, heshouwu, and mushroom three times per day. Another 29 patients were given a placebo. After two months, researchers found that subjects in the treatment group had a 15 percent reduction in fasting glucose.

In another study, 60 Type 2 diabetics were divided into six groups: three placebo groups and three experimental groups. Participants took 1, 3, or 6 grams of cinnamon daily or the placebo. After 40 days, participants in the cinnamon groups had 18 to 29 percent drops in their fasting glucose. They also experienced 20 to 30 percent lower triglycerides, 7 to 27 percent reductions in LDL cholesterol, and 12 to 26 percent lower total cholesterol levels.[17] There were no significant changes in any of the placebo groups. However, all of the patients in the study were also taking oral hypoglycemic (blood sugar-lowering) medications, so it's hard to say for sure in this case if cinnamon was the sole factor in the improvements.

There is a placebo-controlled, double blind trial specific to Cinnulin PF currently under way. The study was designed to determine the effect of supplementation with Cinnulin PF on changes in glucose regulation, lipid profiles (cholesterol, triglycerides, etc.), and overall body composition. But final results won't be available until later this month. So in the meantime, let's take a look at some examples of personal experience with Cinnulin PF.

New ingredient fares well on its own

If Cinnulin PF is independently getting good results, and so is Glucotor, imagine the combined effect. Here are a couple encouraging reports INI has gotten over the past few months from people using Cinnulin PF:

G.P. from Springfield, OH wrote to INI saying "My wife saw an article in Parade magazine and suggested I try Cinnulin PF. I have been taking two capsules daily; the results are in the numbers. The VA Center where I go for treatment asked for a brochure on Cinnulin PF to post on their bulletin board. My doctor is not normally in favor of homeopathic medicine, but she was ecstatic with my results. She had read about cinnamon studies and believes it is a good approach."

And another letter, this one from R.J. in Sanford, FL, said: "I use Cinnulin PF to maintain a healthy blood sugar level. It works! I have used it for a month and I take two tablets before lunch and two before dinner. I also recommend Cinnulin PF to all of my friends who have diabetes."

Same size, same price, better results

Barron did note that some people have a problem digesting the capsules quickly enough to get the blood-sugar lowering effects. The problem, as Barron explains, is that many people, particularly as they get older, have burned out their ability to produce stomach acid. Once you get to that point, you no longer have enough stomach acid to easily break down capsules: It takes so long that the Glucotor can't get in place soon enough to block the receptor sites. But taking the formula out of the capsules lets you bypass that problem. So if you don't get the results you expect, try taking the Glucotor v.2 powder out of the capsules and mixing it with a little applesauce or a small glass of water.

And speaking of capsules, the addition of Cinnulin PF hasn't affected the size or swallow-ability of Glucotor. Barron actually had to create a special encapsulation technique in order to contain the desired dosage of Cinnulin PF along with the other proven ingredients. "After a lot of trial and error and changing how we ground and blended the formula, we found we could get the equipment to fill the standard capsules with the desired dose of the new formula. In other words, we were able to add the Cinnulin PF without having to change anything else."

And that's not the only puzzle they had to solve to get this improved formula to you. Adding Cinnulin PF looked as if it would increase the retail price of the new formula 30 percent. So Barron and Baseline Nutritionals thought they would have to choose whether to raise prices or decrease the number of capsules in each bottle. But they found another alternative—one just about unheard of in the supplement industry: They decided not to do either. So you're getting all the existing benefits of the original Glucotor formula plus the added benefit of Cinnulin PF at no additional cost. This is just another indication of the confidence that Barron and the manufacturers have in this formula.

The recommended dosage for Glucotor v.2 with Cinnulin PF is to one or two capsules five to 10 minutes before eating. If you're currently taking medications for blood sugar, cholesterol, or heart disease, talk to your doctor before trying this formula.

References

Prevent—even reverse—diabetes damage with the vitamin "teacher" breakthrough

1 Albert Einstein College of Medicine of Yeshiva University. Bronx, New York. News Release: Feb 16, 2003

2 Rindi, G. and Laforenza, U. Thiamine intestinal transport and related issues: Recent aspects. Proc. Soc. Exp. Biol. Med. 224: 246-255 (2000).

3 Hammes, H et al. Benfotiamine blocks three major pathways of hyperglycemic damage and prevents diabetic retinopathy. *Nature Medicine* 9:294-299 (2003).

4 Joffe, Dave. "The Inside Story on Why Lipid Solution Thiamine May Benefit Diabetes Patients, Article 122." Diabetes In Control.com, accessed 5/31/04

5 Bitsch R, Wolf M, et al. "Bioavailability assessment of the lipophilic benfo as compared to a water-soluble thiamin derivative." *Ann Nutr Metab* 1991; 35(5): 292-296

6 Wada T, Tagaki H, et al. "A new thiamine derivative, S-benzoylthiamine O-monophosphate." *Science* 1961; 134: 195-196

7 Bitsch R, Wolf M, et al. "Bioavailability assessment of the lipophilic benfo as compared to a water-soluble thiamin derivative." *Ann Nutr Metab* 1991; 35(5): 292-296

8 Loew D. "Pharmacokinetics of thiamine derivatives especially of benfo." *Int J Clin Pharmacol Ther* 1996; 34(2): 47-50

9 Schreeb KH, Freudenthaler S, et al. "Comparative bioavailability of two vitamin B1 preparations: benfo and thiamine mononitrate." *Eur J Clin Pharmacol* 1997; 52(4): 319-320

10 Greb A, Bitsch R. "Comparative bioavailability of various thiamine derivatives after oral administration." Int *J Clin Pharmacol Ther* 1998; 36(4): 216-221

11 Malott, Zachary B. "Benfotiamine—A Miracle? Perhaps when combined with a sensible health regimen." Brentwood Health International (BHI)

12 Brownlee, M. "Benfo blocks three major pathways of hyperglycemic damage and prevents experimental diabetic retinopathy." *Nat Med* 2003; 9(3): 294-299

13 "The effect of intensive treatment of diabetes on the development and the progression of long-term complications in insulin-dependent diabetes mellitus." *N Engl J Med* 1993; 329: 997-986

14 Winkler G, Pal B, et al. "Effectiveness of different benfo dosage regimens in the treatment of painful diabetic neuropathy." *Arzneimittelforschung* 1999;49(3): 220-224

15 Frank T, Bitsch R, et al. "High thiamine diphosphate concentrations in erythrocytes can be achieved in dialysis patients by oral administration of benfo." *Eur J Clin Pharmacol* 2000; 56(3): 251-257

16 Pomero F, Molinar MA, et al. "Benfo is similar to thiamine in correcting endothelial cell defects induced by high glucose." *Acta Diabetol* 2001; 38(3): 135-138

17 Stracke H, Hammes HP, et al. "Efficacy of benfo versus thiamine on function and glycation products of peripheral nerves in diabetic rats." *Exp Clin Endocrinol Diabetes* 2001; 109(6): 330-336

18 Hammes HP, Du X, Brownlee M, et al. "Benfo blocks three major pathways of hyperglycemic damage and prevents experimental diabetic retinopathy." *Nat Med* 2003; 9(3): 294-299

19 Bergfeld R, Matsumara X, Brownlee M. "Benfo prevents the consequences of hyperglycemia-induced mitochondrial overproduction of reactive oxygen species, and experimental diabetic retinopathy."

20 Lin J, Alt A, Brownlee M, Hammes H, et al. "Benfo inhibits intracellular formation of advanced glycation end products in vivo"

21 Holladay, Robert, M.S. Copyright 2003 Robert C. Holladay June 5, 2003 http://www.geocities.com/robholladay99/benfo.html

References

Dodge the sugar bullet—and double your chances of beating this leading killer

1 *Eur J Clin Nutr* 1990; 44(4): 301-6

2 *Prostaglandins Leukot Essent Fatty Acids* 1997; 56 (5): 379-384

3 *Plant Foods Hum Nutr* 1999; 53(4): 359-365

4 *J Biochem (Tokyo)* 1992; 111(1): 109-112

5 *J. Endocrinol* 1999; 163 (2): 207-212

6 *J Ethnopharmacol* 1990; 30: 281-294

7 *J. Ethnopharmacol* 1990; 30(3): 295-300

8 *Bio Environ Sci* 1990 Jun; 3(2): 123-131

9 *Diabetes Care* 2000; 23(1): 9-14

10 *Diabetes Care* 1999; 22(6): 913-919

11 *Int J Obes* 1984; 8(4): 289-293

12 *Diabetes Care* 1999; 22(6): 1-7

13 "Medical Implications of Prickly Pear Cactus," Texas A&M University (www.tamuk.edu)

14 *Gac Med Mex* 1992; 128(4): 431-436

15 Anderson R, et al. "Isolation and characterization of polyphenol type-A polymers from cinnamon with insulin-like biological activity." *J Agric Food Chem* 2004; 52(1): 65-702 ibid

16 Cheng N, Anderson RA, et al. FASEB J 2002 Mar 20;16(4):A647) Cheng N et al. "Hypoglycemic effects of cinnamon, heshouwu & mushroom extracts in Type II diabetes mellitus." *FASEB J* 2002: 16(4): A647

17 Khan A, et al. "Cinnamon improves glucose and lipids of people with type 2 diabetes." *Diabetes Care* 2003; 26(12): 3,215-3,218

Fat-Burning Aids from the Underground

FAT-BURNING AIDS FROM THE UNDERGROUND

Contents

Introduction

In this exciting new report, you'll learn about ...

Safe, Natural Weight Loss: a plan that works <u>with</u> your body to maximize weight loss.

The Fat-gobbling Chemical: It exists in your blood right now! Here's how to wake it up by using simple, little-known "tricks"…as well as a breakthrough new supplement that steps up your body's natural production of this beauty elixir.

Nature's Most Surprising Fat Fighter: This astonishing plant food keeps your fat production down, your energy high, and your appetite in check, safely.

This is the report the obesity industry does NOT want you to read.

If it were up to that industry, you'd still be eating the same old low-cal, low-nutrition, low-flavor foods…or paying hundreds of dollars for the latest dangerous—and almost always useless—prescription weight-loss drug.

The diet and diet-drug industries profit most when you know the least. But we at the Health Sciences Institute are not concerned with the profits of the diet industry. We're concerned only with <u>your education</u> and <u>your control over your own health</u>.

And here's our promise to you: The breakthroughs you'll discover in this report will take your breath away. They're unlike anything else you've ever seen, not only because they're simple and safe but also because they have truly unique properties and abilities. Chances are great that they will help you lose weight with ease.

And you won't have to fight your natural impulse to eat and enjoy food.

The fat-burning aids in this confidential report do NOT make you "hyper" and edgy…they do NOT make you weak and frail…they do NOT deplete your body of precious, essential nutrients…and they do NOT make your body revolt once you stop using them, so that you binge and store fat until you're back up to your original weight!

Before we show you the exciting treatments that you—as a member of the Health Sciences Institute—now have at your fingertips, we want to remind you, briefly, of the weight-loss options available to your friends and neighbors. They probably only know about the weight-loss products offered by the mainstream diet industry. Consequently, they are at the mercy of powerful drug companies, false promises, and dangerous, experimental foods. Losing weight, the mainstream way, can be a very risky endeavor.

You pay them to starve you

Over one-third of adult men and women in America are overweight. And, collectively, we spend more than $33 billion each year trying to lose weight, whether we do it by drinking diet shakes, popping over-the-counter appetite suppressants, joining diet centers, or paying our doctors (and drug companies) for expensive obesity drugs.

That's a lot of money, and a lot of potential harm to our bodies, especially in light of the fact that a full 90 percent of us gain back any weight we lose with the help of these fad diet aids! (And at least one-third gain back more!)

The side effects of these expensive diet aids range from nervousness and muscle loss, to heart problems, kidney trouble, and death.

You also deal with the side effects that hit your wallet, your self-esteem, and your natural, vital energy.

It's no secret: <u>Popular diet fads succeed financially because they fail</u>.

You go on a program, lose weight, gain it back, and return to the program. This is especially true with "quick-loss" diet-center programs.

Restricted, low-calorie diets disturb your metabolism, ultimately sending your body into a starvation mode...until it doesn't want to let go of any more stored energy (fat). And, of course, when you add the stress and anxiety of not being able to enjoy the foods you love to the metabolic trauma you've put your body through, by the time you go off the diet, you virtually have no choice: You have to binge!

All the weight comes back, and then some. So where do you turn? How about to the new prescription obesity drugs?

Weight-loss drugs: Miracle pills or killer capsules?

As an HSI member, you're going to learn some disturbing facts about the fat-burning aids that get promoted...and those that get buried. You'll also see exactly why many safe fat-fighting remedies are driven "underground."

You'll start by getting the answer to this key question: "Who profits from your struggle to lose weight?"

Actually, a better question might be, "Who doesn't profit?"

Drug companies spend up to $400 million—and commit at least seven years of research time—just to get a drug approved by the FDA (and that doesn't even include the billions spent on ads directed to you... and to your doctors). The FDA approval process alone is a time-consuming, resource-draining commitment. And often the entire medical community—drug companies, physicians, hospitals, and medical journals—make major financial commitments every step of the way.

Drug companies offer incentives, "gifts," and kickbacks to encourage physicians to test their drugs on patients. And once a drug is approved... even the physicians can start to profit! Here's a chilling example: a diet powder that made hundreds of doctors $62,000 a piece.

A few years back, the Nutritional Institute of Maryland sponsored a weight-loss plan that used a diet powder it had manufactured. Participating physicians bought the powder diets from the institute and resold them at twice the price. The institute promised that physicians, who enrolled 15 new patients a month and followed them for an average of 3.8 months, would earn $62,000 a year from the sales—not to mention the $6,000 per patient they would earn for performing diagnostic tests to monitor the patients' health.[1]

But that's just the beginning.

The newest weight-loss drugs: more of the same

Drug Name	Company	Chemical Actions	Side Effects
Sibutramine (Meridia)	Knoll Pharmaceutical	Boosts levels of serotonin and another brain chemical, noradrenaline, by inhibiting their reuptake	Elevates blood pressure in susceptible individuals; may cause addiction
Orlistat (Xenical)	Hoffmann-LaRoche	Prevents absorption of fat in the intestine by disabling pancreatic enzymes	Possibly increased incidence of breast cancer; promotes loose stools; causes oily intestinal leakage
Bromocriptine (Ergoset)	Ergo Science	Changes patterns of brain chemicals	Disturbs natural insulin levels
Leptin	Amgen Corporation	Tells the brain to cut back on eating and speeds up metabolism	Possibly contributes to type 2 diabetes

Medical journals are supported by drug companies, which pay hundreds of thousands of dollars to purchase ad space. In fact, these journals are so desperate for this support that they often look the other way when confronted by serious errors in studies and advertisements.

A weight-loss breakthrough?

Remember the "weight-loss breakthrough" called leptin? This little miracle protein was all the rage…for about a month. It was shown to make fat mice lose 30 percent of their weight in just three weeks. Researchers theorized that overweight people were deficient in leptin, a protein that sends the brain messages to "stop eating." Analysts predicted leptin would be the first $10-billion-a-year drug! Researchers raced to develop leptin for use in humans.

Until a few months later, that is, when the researchers made a significant discovery: namely, that obese men and women do, in fact, have plenty of leptin. They just don't have the ability to process its signal properly. The drug was quickly discovered to be no true obesity cure. And more recent research points to leptin as a possible contributor to type 2 diabetes.[2]

And yet the Amgen Corporation, having already invested billions into this faulty treatment, continues to promote it, throwing it into the pool with the other fat-loss drugs you can get today…or will soon be able to get.

Some will promise to speed up your metabolism…some will claim to speed up digestion… and one is supposed to work by preventing absorption of fat in the intestine! But the fat simply leaks out of your body—that's right; it's called "intestinal leakage"—and takes with it vital nutrients, including vitamins D and E, and betacarotene.

Death in a capsule

Remember the "weight-loss miracle" known as "fen-phen?" In 1996, a combination of the diet drugs fenfluramine and phentermine known as fen-phen was introduced to the market—even after reports surfaced during the testing phase that the drugs caused potentially dangerous elevations in blood pressure. Despite the known risks, fen-phen was prescribed to over 18 million people to help them lose weight. Tragically, several people died and hundreds of others suffered serious degeneration of their heart valves before the FDA, in September 1997, finally made it illegal to prescribe the lethal combination.

With that in mind, let's take a look at the newest weight-loss superstar, sibutramine (sold under the trade name Meridia). The FDA's initial response was to deny approval of sibutramine because of concerns that it raised blood pressure. (Sound familiar?) It's rather ironic that FDA approval came swiftly after all, once fen-phen was removed from the market. Whatever the motivations for the approval of sibutramine, it's more important than ever to avoid these weight-loss "wonder" drugs—drugs that can make you sick and even kill you.

Chapter 1

Turn your body into a fat-burning machine with the help of this Ancient Ayurvedic secret

Whether it's a few pounds (or more), there are good reasons for dropping that extra weight. It's not just a matter of being a size smaller. It's protecting your health from the risks that come along with being too heavy—and from going on diet after diet, only to gain weight back.

Here at HSI we scoured our sources to learn more about safe, natural remedies that can aid weight loss—and it's not just by curbing your appetite. Losing weight—and keeping it off—is complicated. It depends on addressing the many contributing factors, like diet, exercise, stress, and nutrition. What we found can help support all of your weight- loss efforts.

Ironically, the promising new remedy we learned about is also among the oldest. It is part of Ayurvedic tradition, practiced in India for centuries.

It's called *garcinia cambogia*, and it's made from the dried rind of the Indian fruit garcinia. Modern research has shown that the active ingredient in garcinia is hydroxycitrate (HCA). HCA can help regulate appetite and maximize carbohydrate utilization.

Emerging research done in lab work and with mice suggest that HCA can help jumpstart metabolism and help burn fat more efficiently. HCA has also been found to help maintain cholesterol and triglyceride levels.

Get that chocolate high while losing weight

We also learned of another all-natural phytochemical that can support the emotional side of your weight-loss efforts. It's called *theobromine*, and its found in, of all things, chocolate. Since the days of the ancient Aztecs, humans have known of the pleasurable effects of chocolate. But until recently, we didn't understand that those effects were caused by theobromine. Luckily, this mild stimulant, which is similar in structure and effect to caffeine, can be isolated from the fat and calories of chocolate. It can make you feel more peaceful and more energized—both things that can aid a weight-loss program.

Natural products that help calm and relax you can also support your efforts to eat healthy. Believe it or not, American Indians have been using an herb called passion flower for centuries to relieve tension and stress. Widely used in Europe as a sedative, passion flower can relieve tension, irritability, and anxiety, as well as improve sleep quality.

Curb cravings and hunger pangs with time-tested herb

We've talked about the emotional aspects of eating, but what about the physical ones? Let's face it, there are physical responses from the body when it desires food. Have you ever heard and felt your stomach growl? And surely you're familiar with those pangs you feel that signal hunger. The problem is, our bodies are conditioned to "ask" for food even if we don't physically need it. That's why herbs that calm the stomach and soothe the intestines can help support your efforts to eat less.

Chamomile is one of the oldest tricks in the book for that purpose. Chamomile tea has been used for years to relieve gas and indigestion and improve digestion. And as an added bonus, chamomile also soothes the nerves and aids sleep.

Finally, you've got to remember that the real object of weight loss is better health, not a certain number on the scale or a certain clothing size. And to that end, nothing is more important than protecting your body from free-radical damage. If you are overweight, chances are you're already putting more stress on your body than you should. And losing weight may actually expose you to even more free radicals—they are released during the breakdown of proteins and fats. Adding *antioxidants* to your diet or supplement program is a good habit to form now and continue even after you reach your weight-loss goal. There are a lot of antioxidants out there—they're found in fruits and vegetables, and in many supplements. If you eat at least five servings of fruits and veggies each day, that's a good start. Blueberries are a particularly rich source of flavonoids, a type of antioxidant that has shown exceptionally strong free-radical fighting properties.

One convenient supplement delivers complete weight-loss support

The good news is that you don't have to hunt down all these individual supplements, or swallow half a dozen pills with each meal. Because there's a formulation that contains all five—garcinia, theobromine, passion flower, chamomile, and an antioxidant-rich blueberry extract—in one convenient capsule.

It's a new product called Weight Guard Plus, with ingredients that are anything but new. Each component of the formula has been used for many years in traditional herbal medicine with no dangerous side effects. And although people are just starting to learn about it, the initial reports are very exciting.

For ordering information, see the Member Source Directory at the end of this report.

Chapter 2

The Olestra experiment: How does it feel to be treated like a lab rat

You've probably already heard of the "breakthrough" fat substitute called Olestra. It's the dieter's dream come true! Eat all the potato chips, cheese puffs, and tortilla chips you want; they're now FAT FREE and just as delicious!

The FDA has approved Olestra, even though it not only causes diarrhea and cramping but also depletes the body of important cancer-fighting nutrients! In order to monitor the long-term effects of Olestra, the FDA has restricted it to certain snack foods. These foods, which will contain a warning label, will be tracked by the FDA to see if Olestra is safe enough to be used more widely.

In other words, this is a colossal experiment: a nationwide study capable of turning all 269 million Americans—including you—into guinea pigs!

In an effort to modify public opinion about the negative effects of Olestra on one's health, Proctor and Gamble (the manufacturer of Olestra) recently sponsored a study that examined its effects when consumed in minute amounts.[1] The results? If you eat just one bag of Olestra chips, *you'll have less diarrhea and cramping than if you eat larger amounts*. Perhaps, like us, you find these conclusions less than reassuring.

And that's just the beginning of the plastic foods and fad diets that will threaten your health in the years to come—foods that may cause bone loss, clogged arteries, and even tumor growth!

But in the middle of this flood of drugs and fake foods, a few safe and successful treatments will emerge to reanimate the lives of those who are lucky enough to hear about them. For example...

Chapter 3

Flirting with perfection: Open the floodgates to the youth elixir in your blood

There's a hormone in your body; the primary function of which is to <u>make you beautiful and strong.</u>

It's no joke! In fact, this hormone has the ability to make you so stunningly strong and vital that as soon as the bodybuilding industry got wind of it, it began researching ways to enhance its production!

This hormone is called, simply, growth hormone (GH). Despite its simple name, GH does a lot more than stimulate growth. It causes tissue to grow and stored energy (fat) to be consumed.

The problem is, however, that nature played a cruel trick on us. As we age, our bodies make less and less of this magic chemical!

When you were a preteen, growth hormone stimulated your skeletal growth. In your teens and early 20s, it reduced stored fat and increased muscle and tissue mass. Sadly, when you hit your mid 20s, GH production started to slow...and it continues to slow to this day.

But you can still tap into it...and turn your body into a youth machine designed to tone you down to your most trim, energetic, and healthy form.

Before we tell you about the different ways to stimulate GH production—including through the use of a new, safe, and powerful GH-stimulating supplement—we want to warn you about the GH stimulants on the market that are, in fact, dangerous.

As we mentioned before, such a powerful youth- and beauty-enhancing chemical is of obvious interest to athletes and bodybuilders. The sports market provided much of the motivation for early research and experimentation with growth hormone. **Anabolic steroids** have been abused for years by people interested in bodybuilding to enhance their athletic performance. But the effects of overuse of artificial substances have often been tragic. Another GH stimulant, **synthetic human growth hormone**, has been available since 1986. Though it is not nearly as dangerous as anabolic steroids, it has been linked to heart disease, and some forms can actually cause antibodies that combat growth hormone.

But here's a simple, safe strategy for stepping up your body's GH production.

• **Eat more cereal grains, nuts, and seeds.** Although these foods contain less arginine than do meat, potatoes, and milk, they also contain less of the amino acids that compete with arginine to cross the brain-blood barrier where they can act on the hypothalamus.

• **Supplement your diet with liquid potassium.** Researchers have discovered a correlation between a reduction in growth hormone and the reduction of dietary potassium. Although you can restore your body's potassium levels by eating natural, whole foods (which have more potassium than sodium), rather than processed foods (which almost always have more sodium than potassium), this is often easier said than done. Liquid potassium tonics are available in health stores.

• **Snack often**…as long as you are snacking on low-sugar, healthful foods! This will keep your blood-sugar level stable. Maintaining stable blood-sugar levels keep your pancreas from producing excess insulin. When there's too much insulin in your blood, your body reacts by producing a chemical called somatostatin. Somatostatin suppresses insulin release…but it also suppresses GH release! This is also a good reason to avoid sugary sweets (especially before bedtime): <u>High sugar snacks prevent the release of GH!</u>

• **If you enjoy exercising, be sure to avoid eating at least two hours before you begin.** To make the best of the small, exercise-induced release of GH, your blood-sugar level must be stable.

• **Make sure you don't eat (again, especially high-sugar foods) within two hours of sleep:** In adults, <u>the largest daily secretion of GH begins about an hour after the onset of deep sleep</u>.

• **Take the dietary amino acid arginine.** As stated before, it has been shown to act on the hypothalamus, which produces a growth-hormone-releasing hormone (GHRH).

HSI Panelist Dr. Allan Spreen told us that arginine is one of the best-known stimulants of the formation of growth hormone by the human body.

As he pointed out, "The injectable HGH (human growth hormone) is risky, as it causes the body to make less of its own, while arginine is the antithesis of that—it causes the body to make *more* of its own. Growth hormone is a wonderful 'youth agent,' and we make less as we age. The effects of rejuvenating the body (its skin, muscles, energy, what-have-you) apparently have been shown to extend to the immune system also."

This safe, proven plan can help you <u>reverse aging,</u> <u>eliminate obesity</u>, and even, according to some experts, convert your body to the Tarzan or Jane musculature into your seventh, eighth, ninth, and even 10th decades!

AN IMPORTANT ASIDE

You're probably already familiar with your body's needs for the essential fatty acids found in olive oil and fatty fish, such as salmon and mackerel. Your body needs these fats in order to maintain good heart health, to keep your cells properly lubricated, and to transport the fat-soluble vitamins, A, D, E, and K. Essential fatty acids make up a major part of the membranes surrounding all cells. Unsaturated fats help your body handle saturated ones. A small amount of fat is an important aspect of healthful dieting.

Chapter 4

Nature's surprising fat fighter: You knew it was good for you...now find out how it helps you lose weight fast!

In a recent obesity study, a group of rats was given a choice of the usual fare of American supermarket snack foods. Remarkably, the animals chose biscuits, chocolates, and marshmallows over regular nutritionally balanced chow.[1]

In 60 days, these ravenous creatures gained an average of 78 grams…which, for a rat, is a lot.

Yes, even a rat can be seduced by foods that are fast, simple, and stimulating.

No one is immune to the temptations of 20th-century, fast-food cuisine. But these foods are not only high in fat and calories and almost devoid of any real nutrition, but also lacking a crucial fat-fighting nutrient—one that you simply cannot afford to be without.

Overcoming the pitfalls of our modern, fat-promoting culture can be as simple as adding to your diet this naturally occurring nutrient that is fat-free, cholesterol-free, calorie-free…and almost completely missing in popular supermarket junk foods: fiber.

It may not be new and exciting… but it IS radical…and it works!

You see, we are bombarded with foods that have been processed so extensively that they are virtually devoid of fiber. Eighty percent of the food we consume in this country is processed. The more the product is refined, the more fiber is removed.

This remarkable nutrient naturally blocks the absorption of fat!

When healthy adults are fed equal amounts of fat in the forms of whole peanuts, peanut butter, and peanut oil, more fat is absorbed from the peanut oil than from the peanut butter, and more from the peanut butter than from the whole peanuts. Why? Fiber blocks the absorption of fat—and hence calories—in the intestines.

The greater your fiber consumption, the higher your caloric waste. Fiber causes a true alteration in digestion and in the absorption of fat. Part of the fat becomes "associated" with fiber, so that it is unavailable for digestion and increases fat excretion.

What's more, when you consume enough fiber, both your small and large intestines contain more watery material. When your bowels are full, you do not feel empty. You stop eating.

What happens when you remove fiber from your foods?

Quite simply, you gain weight much more easily. Here's why.

There's an enzyme in your fat tissue that has the primary function of protecting you from starvation. As soon as any weight loss takes place, this enzyme sends a message to your brain to increase your caloric intake. (Like it or not, this is how our bodies have been responding across the centuries; a reponse more suitable to an age long before the availability of 4,000 foods in your 24-hour supermarket.)

Now, when you eat a natural, high-carbohydrate food that's been stripped of fiber… you're dumping too much sugar into your blood, causing the production of too much insulin.

Too much insulin initiates communication between this enzyme and your brain! In other words, when you eat foods devoid of fiber, you are essentially sending the message "I'm starving!" to your brain, setting in motion the chain of events that leads to slowed calorie burning and more stubborn fat-storage mechanisms.

As you can see, fiber is critical to maintaining a healthy weight.

But how can you get enough fiber in your diet—the 40 to 60 grams required for weight control—when you get only 6 grams of fiber in five heads of lettuce? Two grams of fiber in an apple? Very little fiber in leafy greens? You can't!

Even worse, if you dine out often, or don't have time to buy and prepare fresh, fiber-rich foods on a regular basis, you'll never meet your daily requirement through your diet.

But you can manage a high-fiber intake without making major adjustments to your usual eating regimen.

Fiber supplements contain naturally occurring plant fiber. The formulas are derived from plants that are basically old-fashioned foods but are cloaked in late-20th-century technology.

Note these advantages of fiber supplementation in powder form:

• Grinding fiber into very fine particles makes it more readily digestible.

• Fiber supplements slow digestion, a very beneficial metabolic advantage.

• A high-quality fiber supplement offers standardized pectin, otherwise available only through the consumption of fruits, which may be off-limits to those with blood-sugar problems or those who eat out more than at home.

• Different types of fibers vary in function, and supplements contain a greater variety than you would ordinarily get on your dinner plate even if you chose natural foods as your meal choices.

Taking a fiber supplement on a regular basis assures an ongoing weight-loss advantage on two counts. First, it makes you feel full, which helps control your food consumption. Second, it adds no calories! With supplementation, you can manage a high-fiber intake without adding significant calories— a double whammy to those extra pounds!

It can't be overstated: Fiber is the only component in your daily diet that contains no calories, no fat, and no cholesterol!

An ancient health and beauty secret revived

Two thousand years ago, Hippocrates encouraged high-fiber diets. Fifteen years ago, Denis Burkitt came to this country from England and Africa to share his knowledge about fiber. No one seems to have paid much attention to either of these men of renown.

But the Health Sciences Institute wants you to be fully aware that the addition of a fiber supple-

ment is in your best health interest and is a highly effective way to help lose weight safely and naturally.

There are a few good fiber supplements available. (A good supplement has a blend of natural fibers.) Among them are the following:

• gums, especially guar gum, which moderates sugar absorption better than any other fiber

• psyllium seed husk, which will have a beneficial effect on your glycemic index, your body's response to sugar, and also has great bulking activity

• pectin, mentioned above

Start your fiber supplementation slowly. Work up very gradually to 3 level teaspoons in at least 12 ounces of water. The more water you drink, the better. After two weeks, take the mix twice a day. If necessary, take it three times a day.

It's not necessary to spend a small fortune on fiber, though. You can get a perfectly good fiber supplement containing the above ingredients at your local health-food store.

References

This is the report the obesity industry does not want you to read

[1] "Patients' Diets Which Make Doctors Fat," *Citizen Research Group Health Letter* 1989;5(6): 12
[2] *Science* 1996;274: 1185-88

The Olestra experiment: How does it feel to be treated like a lab rat?

[1] *Journal of the American Medical Association* 1998;279(1): 150-52

Nature's surprising fat fighters: You knew it was good for you…now find out how it helps you lose weight fast!

[1] Tordoff, *American Journal of Physiology* 2002

7 Times Smarter
Stop Memory Loss Dead in its Tracks

7 TIMES SMARTER: STOP MEMORY LOSS IN ITS TRACKS

Contents

As we age, it is very common to observe a gradual decline in mental ability, chiefly memory lapses and difficulty in concentration. These are the result of brain aging: structural changes that take place in our brains as we grow older. Although these changes may be "normal" in the sense that they happen to almost all of us, that does not mean that they are inevitable.

Are you suffering from brain aging?

Signs of brain aging include difficulty in remembering names, directions, words, and appointments; disorientation; memory lapses; and even depression and anxiety. These symptoms can signal the beginning of a breakdown in brain circulation and nerve communication. Even if you've begun to notice subtle signs of decline, it's not too late to take action. With the help of targeted brain nutrients, these connections can be rejuvenated and restored.

Chapter 1

Safe, natural substances nourish your brain and support mental acuity

Safe, natural substances nourish your brain and support mental acuity

There are a number of natural substances you can safely use to support memory and alertness. Modern research has discovered some—and validated others, used for centuries in traditional medicine. Some of these substances work by increasing the amount of oxygen and nutrients available to the brain. Others work more indirectly, boosting the mind by increasing energy levels and supporting mood.

Deliver more super-oxygenated nutrient-rich blood to the brain

For over 20 years, a derivative of the Vinca minor plant (or lesser periwinkle) known as vinpocetine has been used as a prescription medication in Europe and Asia to increase the flow of oxygen to the brain. Research shows that vinpocetine increases cerebral blood flow. This boost in circulation helps support memory and cognitive retention.

Garner more help from gingko

As a powerful vasodilator, ginkgo biloba enhances recall and mental focus in much the same way as vinpocetine—by allowing your blood vessels to transport as much nourishing, oxygen-rich blood as possible to your gray matter.

Free of side effects, Ginkgo biloba also offers headache relief, improvement of vision and hearing, and relief from stress—a key factor in cerebral functioning we discuss more later in this chapter.

Oxygenated blood is critical to the functioning of a healthy brain, but special chemical "messengers" called neurotransmitters are what boosts cognitive performance even higher. Among the various neurotransmitters produced naturally by your body, acetylcholine is the most powerful, and a lack of it can be disastrous. In fact, many forms of age-related cognitive decline have been linked to a deficiency of acetylcholine in the brain.

This is where phosphatidylcholine (lecithin) comes in. Serving as a major structural component of cerebral cells, it plays a vital role in supplying the nutrient "raw materials" your brain needs to maintain production of neurotransmitters like acetylcholine.

Lecithin can also help support short-term memory—things like serial learning, word recognition and recall—in healthy people of all ages.

Boost mental and physical energy

Many people live in a kind of low-energy "fog of the mind" for the majority of their days—especially as they get older. Poor sleep quality, insufficient dietary nutrients, or an overload of mental stress—all can tax your mind into numbness and inefficiency. The link between energy levels and mental acuity is, quite simply, undeniable. And, again, there are natural substances that can raise both levels, helping your brain perform at its very best. Among these are:

DMAE (Dimethylaminoethanol) – What DMAE has that other neurotransmitter-promoting chemicals don't are some well-documented energy enhancement properties.

One study of older adults revealed that 71 percent experienced increased motivation and relief from anxiety.[1] Respondents also reported an increase in mental focus and alertness for several hours following their dosage. And another six-week study reported all of the subjects in the DMAE group experienced an overall improvement in muscle tone, as well as increased mental focus.[2] DMAE is shown to have a positive effect on the ability of the brain's two halves to communicate and interact, which lends verbal and creative abilities a valuable boost.

Trimethylglycine (TMG) – Also known as betaine, TMG is a compound of the amino acid glycine. Supplementing with betaine has been shown to protect liver function. The largest organ in the body, the liver is essential to overall health.

Pantothenic Acid – Well known in the alternative health community and among athletes as a natural stamina-enhancer, pantothenic acid also plays an absolutely crucial role in aiding your body in the production of the vital intelligence-boosting neurotransmitter acetylcholine.

Lift your mood—and improve your memory and cognitive performance

Three safe, natural substances have been shown to be effective mood-elevators and focus-enhancers. They are:

Inositol – This safe and effective natural remedy frees your mind from stress and anxiety—so you can get some real, clear-headed thinking done. Naturally present in your body, inositol is vital for the health of your entire nervous system.

This vital natural substance (which is often grouped with the B-vitamin family) can help promote relaxation and clear thinking.

As an added benefit, inositol can also contribute to energy metabolism. In fact, animal studies have shown a significant, measurable increase in physical activity for up to five hours post-administration.

GABA (gamma-aminobutyric acid) – Research shows that lower than normal levels of GABA in the brain and nervous system are linked to some types of anxiety. An important amino acid-based neurotransmitter, GABA helps to regulate brain and nerve cell functioning, producing a calming and focusing effect that's widely known in the mental health community. Within a well-balanced nervous system, GABA protects against overloads in the neural pathways—and against over-excitement or impulsive lapses in judgment.

N-Acetyl-L-Tyrosine – An amino acid building block, N-Acetyl-L-Tyrosine is an important component in the basic structure of all proteins in the body—and is also the precursor to a pair of neurotransmitters (L-dopa and norepinephrine) that are vital for optimum mental functioning. By boosting production of these vital neurotransmitters, N-Acetyl-L-Tyrosine functions as a natural relaxant—especially if you're under any kind of duress or anxiety.

One new formula provides these nine nutrients—and more

The nine nutritionals discussed above should be available in most health-food stores. Also, North-Star Nutritionals brings all these natural ingredients together in Sense of Mind. And then NorthStar adds in 19 more vitamins, minerals, and antioxidants—providing 28 super-nutrients to help you have the healthy, stress-free body you need for optimum mental acuity and memory.

For information on how to order Sense of Mind, see the Member Source Directory at the end of this report.

Chapter 2

Ancient herb can make your mind young again

New research has led to a breakthrough in the treatment and prevention of brain aging. It's a compound called *huperzine A*, extracted from the Chinese club moss, or *Huperzia serrata*. Used in traditional Chinese medicine for centuries to treat fever and inflammation, this compound has now been shown to bring about significant improvements in cognitive and intellectual performance in patients with Alzheimer's disease and age-related cognitive decline, and it may improve memory and learning in healthy patients as well.

Alan P. Kozikowski, Ph.D., a professor of pharmacology at Georgetown University's Institute of Cognitive and Computational Sciences in Washington, D.C., stated that "according to animal research, it [huperzine A] can actually slow the progression of Alzheimer's disease. In other words, huperzine A has neuro-protective activity, which is really exciting. It makes this supplement really stand out from other treatment modalities."

Researchers at Beijing's Institute of Mental Health conducted a four-week study on huperzine A, administering it to 101 patients with age-associated memory impairment. At the beginning of the four-week study, none of the patients was within the normal range for memory. At the end of the four weeks, however, over 70 percent of those in the huperzine-treated group had improved to within normal memory limits.[1]

How does huperzine A work?

Huperzine A is similar in action to the drugs currently used to treat Alzheimer's disease in that it is a powerful acetylcholine esterase (AchE) inhibitor. AchE is an enzyme that destroys the neurotransmitter acetylcholine and terminates the nerve signal after it has been transmitted. Acetylcholine, which is released at the synapse between two nerve cells, facilitates memory and learning. In some memory disorders, such as Alzheimer's disease, the memory nerve impulse is destroyed before it has been received by the adjacent nerve cell. Thus, by inhibiting AchE, the memory nerve impulse is lengthened in duration, resulting in improved memory and cognitive function.

According to researchers at the Weizmann Institute of Sciences in Rehovot, Israel, and at Georgetown University in Washington, D.C.,

huperzine A is superior in the following ways to the leading drugs licensed for the treatment of Alzheimer's:[2]

- Huperzine A improves learning and memory in mice better than does tacrine.
- Huperzine A acts specifically on AchE in the brain rather than on the AchE found elsewhere in the body.
- Huperzine A does not appear to bind to receptors in the central nervous system, which can cause negative side effects.
- Its effects last 10 to 12 times longer than those of physostigmine and tacrine.
- Huperzine A is less toxic than the leading drugs, even when administered at 50 to 100 times the therapeutic dose.

A marriage of ancient wisdom and leading-edge science

Huperzine A has been used as a prescription drug for treating dementia in China for years. But we've found an innovative formula that augments huperzine with other brain-specific nutrients.

Brain Protex by Nature's Sunshine combines three powerful antioxidants which cross the blood-brain barrier to protect the brain cells. It also contains two nutrients that act as "brain food," namely Ginkgo biloba and phosphatidyl serine. Together, the antioxidants and the nutrients protect the brain from damaging free radicals and boost mental capacity.

Nutrients found in Brain Protex

Phosphatidylserine (PS) is an essential fatty acid that is necessary for optimal brain functioning. It keeps the membranes of the brain cells fluid and pliant, allowing the cells to absorb nutrients more efficiently. It also stimulates the activity of neurotransmitters, the "messenger" chemicals that relay nerve signals from cell to cell, literally helping you think. More than two dozen controlled clinical trials have demonstrated that supplementation with PS greatly improves learning and memory.

In a recent study of 149 people, age 50 or older, who had "normal" age-related memory loss, some study participants took 100 mg of PS three times a day for 12 weeks while the others took placebos. By the end of the experiment, the people taking PS benefited from a 15 percent improvement in learning and other memory tasks, with the greatest benefit coming to those with the greatest impairment. Furthermore, these significant benefits continued for up to four weeks after the patients stopped taking PS. Clinical psychologist Thomas Crook, one of the study's authors, said the study suggests that PS "may reverse approximately 12 years of decline."[3]

In another 12-week study, 51 people (average age: 71) took PS supplements and improved their short-term memory. They could better recall names and the locations of misplaced objects. They remembered more details of recent events and could concentrate more intently.[4]

Ginkgo biloba is a well-known botanical remedy used in the treatment of circulatory diseases, with particular value in the treatment of brain aging. Ginkgo increases circulation to the brain and is a potent antioxidant, helping to prevent free-radical oxidation in the brain.

Rhododendron caucasicum, also known as the "snow rose," grows at altitudes ranging from 10,000 to 30,000 feet in the Caucasus Mountains of the Republic of Georgia (formerly part of the Soviet Union). Many scientists believe Rhododendron caucasicum, which is regularly consumed in the form of Alpine Tea, is a primary cause of Georgians' remarkable longevity. (One census of the Republic's 3.2 million people, identified nearly 23,000 citizens over the age of 100.) Foreign hospitals have used this plant to treat heart disease, arthritis, gout, high cholesterol, blood pressure problems, depression, neuroses, pychoses, and concentration problems.

In the 1950s, Soviet scientists began vigorously researching Rhododendron caucasicum. Over the next four decades, numerous clinical trials explored the therapeutic values of the extract. It proved to be an excellent free radical scavenger (an "ultra-antioxidant" according to some researchers), capable of protecting the body from cell mutations that can weaken the immune system and cause heart disease, cancer, strokes, kidney failure, and emphysema. It exhibited a tremendous ability (stronger than grape seed extract or pine bark extract) to purge harmful bacteria from the body, while allowing good bacteria (probiotics) to remain.

Rhododendron caucasicum, however, demonstrated special abilities to protect and treat the brain. Researchers discovered that its extract bolsters the cardiovascular system, increasing blood supply to the muscles and especially the brain. Studies also demonstrated that Rhododendron caucasicum increases the brain's resistance to unfavorable chemical, physical, and biological imbalances. At the First Lenin Medicinal Institute in Moscow, researchers treated 530 patients with various forms of neuroses and pychoses with Rhodendron caucasicum. Within 11 weeks of treatment, the majority of the patients regained normal conscious thought and demonstrated heightened mental abilities.

Lycopene is a powerful antioxidant found in tomatoes, pink grapefruit, apricots, and watermelon. Observational studies have produced evidence that diets high in lycopene may reduce the risk of cancer, especially tumors in the prostate, colon, stomach, lung, or mouth. Researchers also believe lycopene may help prevent cataracts and macular degeneration (a gradual loss of vision which is the leading cause of blindness among older Americans).

Alpha-lipoic acid is a sulfur-containing fatty acid found in every cell of the body. It is a key component of our metabolic system, helping to convert glucose (blood sugar) into energy to serve the body's needs. It is also a universal antioxidant, capable of eliminating free radicals in water and in fatty tissue.

Lipoic acid has been most commonly used (particularly in Germany) to treat nerve damage caused by diabetes. One randomized, double-blind, placebo-controlled study of 503 individuals concluded that intravenous lipoic acid helped relieve symptoms (pain, numbness, extreme constipation, and irregular heart rhythms) for three weeks.

Researchers now believe lipoic acid may also help retard cataracts and neuro-degenerative diseases, including Parkinson's and Alzheimer's.

Brain Protex can be ordered through The Herbs Place. The recommended dose is two capsules at mealtime twice a day. (See the Member Source Directory at the back of this report for ordering information.)

Could it be Alzheimer's disease?

In its early stages, Alzheimer's can be indistinguishable from "normal" brain aging. But when treated in its earliest stages, its progression can often be dramatically slowed. Recently, very exciting research has shown that nutrients like huperzine A and Ginkgo biloba can even reverse damage that has already occurred.

The cause of Alzheimer's remains unclear, although research reported in recent issues of our *Members Alert* points to several possible culprits, including herpes infection, high homocysteine levels, and aluminum toxicity. As always, a preventive approach is the best defense. You can reduce your risk factors by taking some simple steps now.

Test for heavy-metal toxicity. Hair analysis provides reliable and inexpensive screening for heavy-metal toxicity that can cause serious neurological problems, as well as for mineral imbalances and deficiencies that can affect heart health, bone density, energy metabolism, and other factors. You can work with your physician to obtain one of these tests. One lab we know of is Doctor's Data. For more details see the Member Source Directory.

Reduce your aluminum load. Hair tissue analysis can tell you if your body has stored unhealthy amounts of aluminum. The most common sources of aluminum are cookware, deodorants, baking soda, and antacids. High aluminum levels can be chelated with **malic acid** supplements. The recommended dosage is 500 mg three times a day for no more than three weeks. It is highly recommended that you work with a professional who can monitor your tissue levels and advise you on the protocol. See the Member Source Directory for ordering information.

Keep your homocysteine levels low. This toxic amino acid, also a culprit in the development of heart disease, can increase your risk of Alzheimer's disease. Supplementation with a homocysteine-lowering formula like **CardioSupport** (see the Member Source Directory) can help keep this killer at bay.

Supply brain-targeted nutritional support. Make sure your brain gets an adequate blood supply, sufficient oxygenation, and adequate nutrient support.

If memory lapses, episodes of verbal or spatial disorientation, or personality changes become more frequent or severe, it is important to consult a doctor for a definitive diagnosis.

Chapter 3

Flower power keeps your brain alive

In Alzheimer's patients, chemicals in the brain, called neurotransmitters, go haywire. Neurotransmitters aid communication among brain cells and help electrical impulses jump the tiny gaps (called synapses) between nerves.

In the 1970s, researchers discovered that people with Alzheimer's disease (AD) have low levels of a key neurotransmitter called *acetylcholine* (a-see-tull-KOH-leen). Not only does acetylcholine help brain cells communicate, but it also plays a vital role in memory, learning, and other cognitive functions. In advanced AD patients, acetylcholine levels plunge by 90 percent. At that point, even the personality is affected.

Acetylcholine is produced in an area of the brain called the basal forebrain. Unfortunately, these cells naturally deteriorate with age and are among the first damaged in the early stages of Alzheimer's disease. When these brain cells die, acetylcholine levels drop dramatically—affecting a patient's memory and capacity for learning.

The problem is compounded in AD patients when an enzyme called *cholinesterase* is introduced. Cholinesterase cleans up unused acetylcholine in the brain by breaking it down into its component parts. In a healthy person, this is a natural process. But in AD patients, it can add insult to injury and cripple an already impaired memory by further reducing already low levels of acetylcholine.

The current medications for AD, known as "cholinesterase inhibitors," work primarily by stopping the damage of cholinesterase to optimize the levels of acetylcholine. Aside from harsh side effects, such as liver damage, seizures, and depression, their biggest downfall is that they lose their effectiveness within one year.

Does the snowdrop plant hold the key beyond the temporary relief of drugs?

Working with researchers at Life Enhancement Products, a pioneering nutritional development and research company, we've uncovered dozens of recent clinical trials on a natural flower extract that surpasses the effectiveness of prescription drugs.

Galantamine, an extract from the snowdrop flower, daffodil, spider lily, and other plants, has been traditionally used in Eastern Europe to treat a variety of minor ailments. Current research shows its greatest promise is its ability to bring the progress of AD to a virtual standstill and rejuvenate cognitive function.

Like prescription drugs, galantamine blocks the action of cholinesterase—allowing for greater levels of acetylcholine—and *boosts the production of new acetylcholine* neurotransmitters in the brain.[1]

Furthermore, animal studies have found that galantamine does something else no other drug currently being prescribed can do: It stimulates acetylcholine *receptors*, called *nicotinic receptors*, in the brain—<u>over an extended period of time</u>. In AD patients, these receptors wear out and the brain isn't able to transport acetylcholine from one cell to another. In addition, when nicotinic receptors are healthy and active, they're thought to inhibit the formation of beta-amyloid plaque deposits, a hard, waxy substance that results from tissue degeneration and is often found in the brains of AD patients.[2] While the current AD drugs initially help stimulate the nicotinic receptors as well, the effect isn't long-lasting. Nicotinic receptors appear to become desensitized to most drugs over time—often within a year—thus making them ineffective in this respect. Unlike AD drugs, galantamine stimulates nicotinic receptors without appearing to cause desensitization when used for an extended period of time.[3]

Increase memory and cognitive function—and keep it

Scientists in Auckland, New Zealand, found that AD patients in several studies (with 285 to 978 patients taking 24 milligrams of galantamine per day for three to six months) achieved significant improvements in cognitive symptoms and daily living activities as compared to a placebo-treated control group. They also found that galantamine delayed the development of behavioral disturbances and psychiatric symptoms. After 12 months of treatment, patients using galantamine maintained their cognitive and functional abilities.[4]

Researchers in Belgium conducted a study with 3,000 AD patients enrolled in one of five randomized, controlled, double-blind groups. Various levels of galantamine were tested (16, 24, and 32 milligrams per day) against placebos, and in every study the galantamine-treated patients maintained their cognitive abilities while the placebo-treated subjects experienced significant deterioration.

Prior to entering each of the five studies, patients were evaluated according to the cognition portion of the Alzheimer Disease Assessment Scale. Each subject's performance was assessed in 11 areas measuring memory and orientation. A score of zero meant the patient made no errors, while a top score of 70 meant he suffered from profound dementia. Results from the patient evaluations showed that moderately severe AD patients treated with galantamine had a seven-point advantage over similarly afflicted subjects in the placebo groups. Researchers found that the optimum dosage of galantamine was 24 milligrams per day. Groups treated with 32 milligrams demonstrated no additional improvement in their cognitive abilities.[5]

In another multicenter, double-blind trial, galantamine delayed the progress of the disease throughout a full-year study. Conducted at the University of Rochester Medical Center, 636 patients with mild to moderate AD were given galantamine or a placebo for six months. At the end of the period, patients taking galantamine experienced improved cognitive function in relation to the placebo group. Patients taking 24 milligrams of galantamine improved by 3.8 points. Additionally, based on clinician and caregiver interviews, the galantamine group performed significantly better in the completion of daily activities and exhibited fewer behavioral disturbances. Moreover, the benefits of galantamine are long-lasting. Baseline cognitive scores and daily function continued to be high when retested at 12 months for patients taking 24 milligrams of galantamine.[6]

Not only that, but researchers have also determined that galantamine regulates the release of the neurotransmitters glutamate, gamma-aminbutyric acid, and serotonin—all of which play a vital part in proper memory function.[7]

Galantamine fights mental deterioration and increases memory and cognitive abilities— even in Alzheimer's victims

A recent series of comprehensive clinical trials unveiled some exciting new potential for galantamine, not only for treatment but also for prevention and overall cognitive function.

Researchers once thought AD patients who inherited two copies of the apolipoprotein E gene (*APOE* genotype) believed to cause AD wouldn't benefit as much from cholinesterase inhibitors as other AD sufferers. In four international placebo-controlled clinical trials lasting from three to 12 months, researchers at the Janssen Research Foundation in Belgium studied 1,528 AD subjects with two copies of the APOE genotype and tested the efficacy of galantamine. While those with two copies of the specific gene had an earlier onset of AD symptoms, they received equal benefit from galantamine supplementation as compared with those who had AD from other gene types. So regardless of the genetic origin of AD, galantamine improved cognitive abilities and capacity to handle normal day-to-day activities.[8]

In addition to forgetting things and not being able to draw on previous learning experiences, AD patients have an impaired ability to learn new tasks. In recent animal tests, researchers found that galantamine modifies the nicotinic receptors so there's an increased release in the amount of acetylcholine in addition to acting as an acetylcholinesterase inhibitor. Scientists concluded that daily administration of galantamine over a period of 10 days results in an increase of conditions that are known to augment learning opportunities in AD patients.[9]

Put all these characteristics together, and the overall result for AD patients—as dozens of clinical trials prove—is that the disease slows *dramatically* and the victim's memory can stabilize and even improve. The latest studies add to the growing body of evidence on the preventative potential of galantamine and its ability to rejuvenate your overall learning and performance.

Rescue your brain—cell by cell— starting today

The proof of galantamine's effectiveness in treating AD is so impressive that it's already being put to use around the world. Under the market name Reminyl,® it has been used widely in 15 European countries. In 1999, Janssen Pharmaceutica submitted Reminyl to the FDA for approval; the FDA sanctioned it for use in AD patients the beginning of March 2001.

But approval by the FDA is only the first step on a long path to getting help for the patient. According to the National Academy of Sciences' Institute of Medicine, important research discoveries can take as long as 17 years before information about them filters down to doctors and hospitals. And even if your doctor knows about a supplement or drug, your HMO or insurance company might not approve it because of the expense. Or they may feel you don't have sufficient need for a particular drug. Regardless of the potential benefits, mountains of red tape and bureaucratic nonsense might prevent you from getting the products you need.

The good news is you don't have to wait. While the pharmaceutical giants, insurance companies, and HMOs fight to get their extracts packaged, marketed, and distributed, you can protect your memory and intellect and put a stop to the advance of AD with the natural form of galantamine.

It's currently available from Life Enhancement Products in a formula called GalantaMind,® which combines galantamine with vitamin B_5 and choline. Refer to page 10 for purchasing information.

Galantamine does have a few minor side effects: nausea, vomiting, and diarrhea. However, they can be significantly reduced and even eliminated by taking smaller initial dosages and working up to the full dosage over a week's time.

The mountain of evidence on the benefits of galantamine for Alzheimer's patients is undeniable. Anyone battling this difficult disease should consider asking his/her doctor about it.

Member Source Directory

Brain Protex, The Herbs Place; 27 Fleetwood Dr, Palmyra, VA 22963; tel. (866)580-3226; www.theherbsplace.com/brain.html.

CardioTotal, Gold Shield Healthcare Direct; 1501 Northpoint Parkway, Suite 100, West Palm Beach, FL 33407; tel. (800)474-9495; www.goldshieldusa.com.

Hair Toxic Element Exposure Test, Doctor's Data, 3755 Illinois Ave, St. Charles, IL 60174; www.DoctorsData.com. *Note: Test must be ordered by a physician.*

GalantaMind (Galantamine), Life Enhancement Products, Inc; P.O. Box 751390, Petaluma, CA 94975-1390; tel. (800)534-3873 or (707)762-6144; www.life-enhancement.com.

Sense of Mind, NorthStar Nutritionals, P.O. Box 970, Frederick, MD 21705; tel. (888)856-1489; www.northstarnutritionals.com. Ask for Code: MBR009.

Please note: HSI receives no compensation for providing editorial coverage for the products that appear in this report. HSI is a subsidiary of the same holding company as NDI Solutions, the distributor of NorthStar Nutritionals, RealAdvantage and Pure Country Naturals supplements.

HSI verifies all product information when reports are written; however, pricing and availability can change by the time reports are delivered. We regret that not all products are available in all locations worldwide.

The above statements have not been evaluated by the U.S. Food and Drug Administration. These products are not intended to diagnose, treat, cure, or prevent any disease.

References

Safe, natural substances nourish your brain and increase mental acuity

[1] *Journal of the American Geriatrics Society* 1977;25(6): 241-44

[2] Pelton, Ross and Taffy Pelton, "Mind Food and Smart Pills," Doubleday Books, 1989, p 79

Ancient herb can make your mind young again

[1] *Neuropsychopharmacology* 1994;10(3S)/part I: 763s

[2] *Journal of the American Medical Association* 1997;277(10): 776

[3] *Neurology* 1991;41(5): 644-49

[4] *Psychopharmacology Bulletin* 1992;28(1): 61-66

Flower power keeps your brain alive

[1] *Behavioral Brain Research* 2000;113(1-2): 11-19

[2] The Newsletter of the Memory Disorders Project at Rutgers-Newark, Winter 2001

[3] *Dementia and Geriatric Cognitive Disorders* 2000;11(Suppl 1): 11-18

[4] *Drugs* 2000;60(5): 1095-1122

[5] *Dementia and Geriatric Cognitive Disorders* 2000;11(Suppl 1): 19-27

[6] *Neurology* 2000; 54(12): 2269-76

[7] National Institute on Aging

[8] *Dementia and Geriatric Cognitive Disorders* 2001;12: 69-77

[9] *Behavioral Brain Research* 2000;113(1-2): 11-19

Secret Germ Antidote KNOCKS OUT FLU IN 8 HOURS

Secret germ antidote knocks out Flu in 8 hours

Russian immune booster giving people their lives back

In 2002, National Geographic published an article that related the details of how the Chernobyl nuclear accident destroyed a nearby anthrax research lab, releasing live anthrax into the wind and affecting villages for more than 60 miles.

What National Geographic didn't cover is what happened in response to this disaster. The Russian military directed classified researchers at the State Scientific Center Research Institute of Highly Pure Biopreparations, located in Saint Petersburg, Russia, to develop protection against such biological warfare agents.

Starting in 1980, the team studied more than 600 products. Only one exhibited effectiveness, low cost, and high safety. The Russian microbiologists discovered a special strain of lactobacillus bacteria with powerful immune-protecting properties. Lactobacillus occurs naturally in your nose, mouth, throat, and intestines.

With all the recent hype about probiotics, you've probably heard about the benefits of lactobacillus. Well, take that concept and put it through special training and you get the powerful immune-boosting formula developed by the Russian scientists—a formula that helped one pharmacist give his daughter back a normal life.

Knock out flu in less than a weekend

I recently spoke with that pharmacist, John Sichel. He told me that, in his profession, he comes into contact with quite a few product manufacturers—and all sorts of product samples. Most of the time, this is just a run-of-the mill part of his job. But in 1999 he received a sample of this supercharged lactobacillus formula. When Sichel's daughter, Pamela, came down with the flu that winter, he gave her the sample. It completely knocked out her flu symptoms in just eight hours. Sichel was impressed, but he didn't think much more about the supplement again until several months later, when he received a heart-wrenching call from Pamela.

For several years she had been experiencing symptoms of hepatitis C—brain fog, fatigue, depression, and flu-like symptoms that would not go away. Now, though, her doctor told her she had a viral load of about 250,000 (a healthy person would typically have a viral load of 0), and her immune system just wasn't handling the attack.

Sichel remembered giving her the Russian immune-boosting product to beat the flu and how well it had worked. So he suggested she try the same formula again, although he had no idea if it could pack the same punch against the more serious, aggressive illness his daughter was facing this time. But to his astonishment, once again, the virus was no match for the product. Within just a few months, all of Pamela's hepatitis symptoms were completely gone. She began taking the formula daily—her viral load quickly normalized, and she remains in good health today.

This time, he was so impressed that what had been "just another product sample" quickly became the new focus of his career.

After 50 years working in the pharmaceutical industry, Sichel understood that unless the product became mainstream—accepted under the watchful eye of U.S. agencies—there was a good chance that his daughter's deliverance would not be available to her, or anyone else, in years to come.

To ensure that this didn't happen, he went to pretty extreme measures. He learned enough Russian to be able to effectively communicate with the product's developers and actually traveled from his home in Boulder, Colorado to Russia. Sichel spent the next three years working with the original formulators to devise a plan of action to manufacture this extraordinary product in the USA.

Now, this product, known by many aliases—Lactoflor, Matrix E., Preparate, Extrabiolate, and its current moniker Del-Immune™—is not only available in this country, but it's also 10 times more powerful than the original formulation.

Breaking down walls to build stronger immunity

When he arrived in Russia, Sichel's first priority was to learn as much about the product as possible. The Russian microbiologists explained to him that they'd worked with scientists in Bulgaria to supercharge the lactobacillus agent. The Bulgarians showed the Russians how to break the cell walls of this potent lactobacillus, because their research proved that the immune-protecting properties in lactobacillus exist as proteins inside the cell.

Unless the cell wall is broken, our immune systems are unable to "see" these proteins, which are necessary for a dramatic immune response. Once the cell wall is successfully broken, the resulting cell pieces are called "cell wall fragments." Cell wall fragments have been found to contain highly active proteins, amino acids, and complex sugars that account for the effect upon the immune system. So the researchers used these fragments to create a supplement by freeze-drying them, crushing them into a fine powder, and encapsulating them.

Small quantities of this product were brought to the United States, and Sichel was one of the few people who received samples. Subsequently, nothing came of this technology until Sichel formed a partnership with the Russian researchers.

Fans of the original have even higher praise for U.S. version

Since the manufacturing technology was transferred to the U.S., further refinements, involving innovative culture nutrition and precisely controlled manufacturing procedures, have produced significant improvements in potency over the original Russian product.

The U.S.-made product is estimated to be 10 to 30 times more potent than the Russian counterpart—with three times more proteins within the cell walls. This is due to over a year of diligence by the U.S. team, using the lab's experience in culture nutrition and modern technology to produce and test the product. They paid special attention to laboratory analysis, DNA formatting, and the development of good manufacturing practice (GMP) standards. Currently, quality control using DNA and other contemporary analysis methods ensures that every batch of Del-Immune is pure and identical.

Sichel told me that many of the original product users were asked to try the new U.S.-made version and report their impressions. More than 50,000 doses of the new Del-Immune product were evaluated in human subjects for comparison, and the results were great news for all of us. Since each capsule is equal to more than two capsules of its predecessor, many users who were taking two or more capsules a day were able to cut their dose in half, saving money in the process. The higher potency also appeared to decrease the amount of time it takes for the product to "kick in" and start working.

He explained that typical use for Del-Immune is to provide effective, reliable, safe, and immediate immune system support. Users have provided anecdotal reports with its application in flu, West Nile virus, colds, coughs, bronchitis, fatigue, hepatitis C, certain skin infections, yeast, non-healing fractures, constipation, and side effects of chemo and radiation therapies. Essentially, Del-Immune acts like your body's specially-trained secret virus-fighting agent.

You can't get this immune boost from yogurt alone

To understand how Del-Immune works, you need to understand some basics of your immune system. According to James L. Wilson, N.D., Ph.D., "The immune system comprises an innate immune system and an acquired immune system. A portion of this elaborate network of immune defense is functional at birth; this is the innate immune system. When called upon, it moves with great speed. A second immune system develops as the body interacts with the environment (and reacts to such influences as vaccination); it is the acquired immune system and works slowly. The host is protected by both the innate and the acquired immune systems, working together."

White blood cells, called T-cells, are a part of the innate immune system. The T-cells first act as a command center that issues combat orders. Then, this part of the immune system fights viral and bacterial invaders directly—think of it like hand-to-hand combat.

Meanwhile, the B-cells of the acquired immune system act as the artillery. Keeping a safe distance from the invader, B-cells deliberately fire round after round of antibodies toward the perceived enemy without having direct contact with it.

Del-Immune helps the two systems work together more effectively in viral combat situations.

Wilson explained that he was so impressed by this idea and his own clinical experiences, he started investigating the scientific basis for immune enhancement with lactobacilli cell walls and cell wall fractions. Of the various combinations commercially available, the cell wall fractions of specific strains of Lactobacillus bulgaricus (L. bulgaricus) appear to be the most potent. One of the significant discoveries the U.S. team made was to identify this strain using modern technological advances— technology not available to the Russian lab at the time of original strain identification.

Wilson explains that the difference in performance between "these immune enhancing strains of L. bulgaricus and yogurt cultures or the common lactobacilli preparations sold for intestinal bacteria replacement is...vast."

Your secret agent in the fight against colds and flu

I told you about Pamela Sichel's fast relief from the flu and from hepatitis C after taking Del-Immune, but she isn't alone. I spoke to several people who swear by its protective effects.

After taking Del-Immune at her daughter's recommendation as a quick fix for her flu symptoms, one woman began taking it as a daily immune-support supplement. As a fifth-grade teacher, she was constantly battling whatever bug her students were passing around. But since she started taking Del-Immune daily, she told me, she has yet to bring home any illnesses from school.

Perhaps even more striking is 56-year-old Matthew R.'s story. He told me that Del-Immune sent the reinforcements his system badly needed to heal after major surgery and cancer treatment: "Two years ago I had two major surgeries. One was to remove a tumor, and, unfortunately, a type of lymphoma cancer was found. Lymphoma affects the immune system and I caught a very bad cold after leaving the hospital. I got down to 112 pounds from 140 pounds and was very weak. John Sichel heard about my illness and offered me some packets of Del-Immune powder. I have taken one dose every day since. Only once in two years did I get sick. That was when I ran out of it... As soon as I started Del-Immune again, things got better. No more colds or flu. I have made sure I don't run out again, as I am convinced the Del-Immune is keeping my immune system working."

Primetime cover-up?

In the course of my research, I had a chance to watch a never-aired documentary from a major network news program on Del-Immune. According to the tape, it appears that Del-Immune is not just for colds, flus, and biological pathogens; if your body's immune system needs support, it seems to benefit from this product.

In 1992, after the Cold War, the product—no longer classified—was used clinically in the treatment of breast, lung, and liver cancers, serious hospital-type infections, and contagious disease at the State Cancer Hospital in St. Petersburg, Russia. The product was also used to boost the immune systems of patients undergoing chemo and radiation therapies, allowing the patients to complete their therapies without the usual debilitating effects. Numerous Russian studies document the remarkable cancer-related uses of this secret agent. The doctors reported that the patients on Del-Immune looked and felt better and had more energy.

With such promising reports and potential benefits, it's tough to fathom why the piece never aired, but if I had to guess, I'd say it probably had something to do with the all-too-familiar red tape so many effective natural treatments encounter when they're brought to the public. But despite the suppressed news coverage, Del-Immune is now available in this country, and, as you've read, it's already becoming the answer to many people's immune concerns.

Fast relief without the side effects

Del-Immune offers both consistent long-term support and immediate support. The recommended daily dose as a dietary supplement is one to three capsules daily, or as directed by a healthcare provider. The fast-acting remedy dose—two capsules immediately, followed by an additional two capsules 12 hours later—should be taken at the first sign of cold or flu.

After taking Del-Immune, you can expect the boost of immune support to begin in approximately six to eight hours. Relief is often as fast as 24 hours but varies for each person.

There are virtually no reported side effects and it is shown to be very safe—even at high doses of up to 15 grams per day. According to the manufacturer, during testing, massive dosages—50 to 100 times the suggested dose—caused gastric upset in some subjects. Dr. Elin Ritchie, a medical doctor with a practice in Taos, New Mexico, remarks that, "I have used Del-Immune in more than 20 patients in the last few months, since it became available to me. None of the patients have experienced any side effects."

Many of the testimonials in the never-aired documentary mentioned that they were especially confident in the safety of the product. And because it is grown in a special media, not cultured in milk, some lactose intolerant users have reported they experience no problems taking it.

See the Member Source Directory on page 110 for complete ordering information.

HSI's immune-boosting all-stars

All too often these days, just as you find a natural alternative that works—poof! It's no longer available, but there are three others I wanted to mention.

These few products aren't necessarily "late breaking news," but they are effective in helping boost your immune system. And in a time where our effective natural options are dwindling fast, it's more important than ever to be aware of what we still do have access to.

N-acetylcysteine (NAC) is a naturally occurring derivative of the amino acid cysteine. Your body uses NAC to manufacture another compound called glutathione, which acts as a master antioxidant and liver detoxifier. As such, glutathione plays a critical role in supporting the immune system—fighting disease and protecting the vital systems of our bodies.

Glutathione stores can be depleted by injury, strenuous activity, chronic disease, or radiation exposure. Supplementing with NAC will help restore and maintain optimum intracellular (inside the cell) glutathione levels.

According to one human trial, NAC significantly increased immunity to flu infection. Over a six-month period, only 29 percent of those people taking NAC developed symptoms of the flu, vs. 51 percent of those taking a placebo.[1]

NAC is widely available in health-food stores and through mail-order companies.

The second featured product is ImmPower (AHCC). AHCC is an extract of a unique hybridization of several kinds of medicinal mushrooms known for their immune-enhancing abilities. On their own, each mushroom has a long medical history in Japan, where their extracts are widely prescribed by physicians. But when combined into a single hybrid mushroom, the resulting active ingredient is so potent that dozens of rigorous scientific studies have now established AHCC to be one of the world's most powerful—and safe—immune stimulators.

Since 1987, various clinical trials conducted in Japan have demonstrated that AHCC has the ability to support normal immune function. More than 700 hospitals and medical clinics in Japan recommend AHCC as part of a regular immune maintenance program. It's available in America as Imm-Power™ AHCC®.

Typically, each soft-gel capsule contains 300 mg of AHCC. Dosage recommendations range as follows: For maintenance of general health and prevention of disease, 1 to 3 grams per day; for treatment or prevention of cancer drugs' side effects, 3 to 6 grams per day.

Our third standout—lactoferrin—has literally been around forever. In fact, lactoferrin, an iron-binding protein in breast milk, was the very first immune booster. It has two specific functions: First, it binds to iron in your blood, keeping it away from cancer cells, bacteria, viruses, and other pathogens that require iron to grow. And it also activates very specific strands of DNA that turn on the genes that launch your immune response.

Numerous studies on rats as well as patient case histories have documented the benefits of lactoferrin in helping to combat many types of viral and bacterial illnesses, as well as malignancies.

The general recommended dose is 100 milligrams each day, taken at bedtime.

For product information and how to order, see the Member Source Directory on page 110.

Member Source Directory

Del-Immune, Pure Research Products, 6107 Chelsea Manor Court, Boulder, Colorado, 80301; ph. (888)466-8635; www.del-immune.com. A 30-capsule bottle cost US$19.50 plus shipping. Discounts offered when ordering in bulk.

ImmPower (AHCC), Harmony Co.; tel. (888)809-1241; www.theharmonyco.com. A 30-capsule (500-mg) bottle is $49.95 plus shipping.

Immunoguard (lactoferrin), Gold Shield Healthcare, 1501 Northpoint Parkway, Suite 100, West Palm Beach, FL 33407; tel. ((800)474-9495; www.goldshieldusa.com.

References

1 "Attenuation of influenza-like symptomatology and improvement of cell-mediated immunity with long-term N-acetylcysteine treatment," *Eur Respir J.* 1997; 10(7):1,535-1,541

Report 12

Today's Most Vital Health Secrets

TODAY'S MOST VITAL HEALTH SECRETS

Contents

Chapter 1

Australian breakthrough against asthma and allergies

Australia has the highest incidence of asthma in the world. One out of every four Australian children is afflicted with the disease. But a remarkable new preparation, developed by a private Australian research company, is causing a small revolution. In many cases, asthmatics have been able to throw away their inhalers after a few weeks, sparing themselves the potentially deadly risk of steroid medications.

The natural preparation causing such a stir in Australia is Oralmat, a patented extract of Secale cereale, more commonly known as ryegrass. This completely non-toxic and pleasant-tasting liquid is administered under the tongue (three drops, two or three times a day), allowing the active ingredients to be absorbed directly through the mucous membranes of the mouth, bypassing the digestive system.

Researchers report that adult asthmatics get significant relief—often enough that they can reduce or eliminate other asthma medications—after using Oralmat drops for three to four weeks. In children, the effect is often much more rapid.

Allergies, infections, and immune disorders also improve

But asthma is just one of dozens of conditions that reportedly improve with Oralmat. Scores of anecdotal and clinical reports indicate success against allergies; colds; influenza; chronic fatigue syndrome; viral, fungal, and bacterial infections; HIV-related complications; diabetes; multiple sclerosis; Gulf War syndrome; and other maladies. In five years of clinical use, not a single adverse response has been reported.

Dr. Chris Reynolds was the first doctor to use the extract in a clinical practice. In an article for the *Australian Naturopathic Practitioners and Chiropractors Association Journal*, he admitted his initial surprise at Oralmat's effectiveness:

"Having never prescribed an herbal medication during my 25 years as a doctor, the efficacy and broad spectrum of activity of this product surprised me. The manufacturers appear to have achieved an important medical breakthrough."[1]

Oralmat's impressive results

Dr. Reynolds has used Oralmat with hundreds of patients, accumulating an astonishing catalog of beneficial outcomes:

- In chronic fatigue syndrome, symptoms usually abate within seven to 10 days.
- Patients with multiple sclerosis experience a "dramatic reduction in fatigue" and fewer and less-severe relapses.
- Diabetics, both insulin-dependent and non-insulin-dependent, report lower blood-glucose levels and a reduction in insulin requirements.
- Cold and flu symptoms frequently disappear within hours of administration.
- Asthmatics frequently are able to discontinue prescribed medication after a few weeks of use.
- Hayfever and allergic rhinitis—even severe, chronic cases—improve rapidly, sometimes within minutes of administration. Rapid drainage of congested sinus passages relieves sinus headaches.

"The extract appears to be a powerful immuno-modulator," Dr. Reynolds concludes. "It is inexpensive, it's not unpleasant to take, and administration is simple. It could replace many traditional medications, eliminate many adverse reactions, and palliate or cure multitudes."

Other doctors from around the world have reported dramatic improvements in patients with chronic fatigue syndrome, Gulf War syndrome (GWS), chronic hepatitis, herpes infections, and HIV/AIDS.

Philip Princetta, D.C., of Atlanta, Georgia, also reports impressive results with allergy and asthma patients:

"The Southeast United States, and Atlanta, Georgia, in particular, is a well-known allergy area of the world. The damp tropical climate allows for a plethora of allergens. Even some of my worst allergy patients responded very well to the drops and suffered a minimum of 50 percent less this past spring."

The sum of its parts

Chemical analysis reveals a few active ingredients: phytoestrogens (including genistein and matiresinol), coenzyme Q_{10}, squalene, and beta 1,3 glucan. Each of these constituents is known to have significant health benefits.

Although the presence of these compounds provides some insight into Oralmat's powers, many questions remain unanswered. The manufacturers do not specify what amounts of these immune-stimulating substances are found in the product, but they appear to be relatively low. Other benefits, such as relief of allergies and reduction of insulin dependence, would not ordinarily be expected from these constituents—at any potency.

The extraordinary anecdotal reports about Oralmat have prompted investigators at John Hunter Hospital in Newcastle, Australia, to conduct more rigorous, placebo-controlled trials. The first, begun last fall, will evaluate the effectiveness of Oralmat as an asthma medication, alone and in combination with prescription medications. The trial has not yet been completed, but researchers are reporting "extremely promising" preliminary results. A trial on chronic fatigue syndrome is scheduled to begin next year.

A spokesperson for the manufacturer of Oralmat points out that "such strictly supervised medical testing of natural herbal remedies only happens when the evidence of their success has reached a level that the conservative medical profession can no longer ignore."

For more information on ordering Oralmat, see the Member Source Directory at the back of this report.

Chapter 2

Turn back the clock with nature's new fountain of youth
Six times stronger than the anti-aging secrets of the stars

Imagine if the fountain of youth really existed. Imagine if you could wash yourself in its healing waters and walk away feeling and looking like you were in your prime again. What if you didn't have to worry about cancer, hypertension, or other age-related diseases?

Just think about it…would you live your life differently? Would you spend more time visiting friends, outdoors, or at the beach? Would you get started on all those projects around the house that you never have the energy for? Would you lead a more active love life, take up a new hobby, change careers, or just play with your grandchildren on the floor once in a while?

This doesn't have to be just a fantasy. You can now slow, halt, and even reverse the effects of aging on your body. Health Sciences Institute has recently uncovered what could be the most powerful anti-aging supplement ever developed. This breakthrough has been proven to literally reverse the body's aging process by rebuilding old, damaged cells. With this powerful, life-changing panacea you can:

- Protect your cells from degenerative ailments like heart disease, MS, and Parkinson's disease
- Improve chronic age-related conditions like arthritis and osteoporosis
- Wipe away wrinkles and liver spots
- Feel an overwhelming sense of well-being throughout the day
- Regain muscle mass and mobility in your limbs
- Improve the luster and vitality of your hair, nails, and skin
- Sleep through the night and wake up feeling alert and energized
- Boost your immune system

H-3 Plus promises all this and more. It's the next generation of an anti-aging formula developed in Romania almost 50 years ago and heralded by the TV show *60 Minutes* back in 1972. The difference is, H-3 Plus is *six times stronger 15 times longer* than the original Romanian formula …and it lasts.

This cutting-edge compound has been developed by a distinguished think-tank of scientists and researchers—including HSI panelist, acclaimed author, and nutritional expert, Ann Louise Gittleman, N.D., C.N.S, M.S. It's just been patented in the United States, so there aren't many clinical studies yet. However, the initial results collected by Gittleman and her associates are so astonishing, we wanted to tell you about it immediately so you don't have to wait years for Mike Wallace to get wind of it.

The Romanian anti-aging miracle similar to an ingredient every dentist uses

The story of H-3 Plus actually begins almost 100 years ago in Austria. Procaine—the primary active ingredient in H-3 Plus—was first discovered in 1905 by biochemist Dr. Alfred Einhorn while he was looking for a non-toxic, non-addictive anesthetic. At the time, cocaine was primarily used, but its negative characteristics were becoming apparent and its use was going to be outlawed. Procaine (very similar to novocaine) became a safe alternative anesthetic.

Nearly 50 years later in 1949, Dr. Ana Aslan of the National Geriatric Institute in Bucharest, Romania, discovered Procaine's anti-aging properties virtually by accident. Familiar with its anesthetic properties, Dr. Aslan began to inject her elderly arthritis patients with Procaine. To her surprise, not only did her patients experience decreased pain and increased mobility, they also began to experience overwhelming physical and mental improvements.

Dr. Aslan called her new discovery GH-3 and began a massive series of clinical trials that studied the effects of Procaine on 15,000 patients between ages 38 and 62. The study included over 400 doctors and 154 clinics, and at that point may have been the largest double-blind trial ever undertaken.

Procaine repairs the damage of old age, toxins, and disease from the inside out

By the time most of us reach 30, our bodies stop reproducing cells at the rate they once did. We literally lose more cells than we gain. And the cell membranes begin to erode and don't absorb nutrients as efficiently. New scientific evidence even suggests that many degenerative diseases—such as cancer, MS, and Parkinson's—are manifestations of damage to these cell membranes.[1]

Dr. Aslan and her research team found that Procaine works by penetrating old or damaged cell membranes and repairing the erosion caused by old age, disease, toxins, food additives, and stress. Bathed in this powerful elixir, cells in the body are then able to receive nutrients and vitamins and expel toxins effectively. This makes for a healthier—and younger—body, from the inside out.

In 1956, Dr. Aslan presented her findings to the European Congress for Gerontology meeting in Karlsruhe, West Germany. While her claims were initially met with skepticism, Aslan's astonishing conclusions could not be ignored for long:

- Close to 70 percent of GH-3 patients never contracted a disease
- Overall, the death rate in the GH-3 group was more than 5 times lower than the placebo

group over 3 years
- Patients were less prone to infectious diseases and seasonal influenza
- Reduction of sick days off work by almost 40 percent
- Joint mobility improved in 56 percent of cases[2]

While not a cure to any single disease, GH-3 was proven to target and improve many common chronic diseases and conditions including:

Acne
Arthritis
Decreased sex drive
Dementia
Depression
Emphysema
Excessive cholesterol
Failing memory
Heart disease
Hodgkin's disease
Hypertension
Lethargy
Liver spots
Migraine headaches
Multiple sclerosis
Osteoporosis
Parkinson's disease
Peptic ulcers
Poor circulation
Rheumatism
Sickle cell anemia
Sleep disorder
Varicose veins

60 Minutes uncovers Dick Clark's anti-aging secret

During most of the 1960s, GH-3 fought its way through U.S. federal regulations. Then in 1972, Mike Wallace of *60 Minutes* did an investigative piece on this underground anti-aging formula and much of the western world finally took notice. Since it was first developed, over 100 million people in more than 70 countries have used Dr. Aslan's formula. Hundreds of thousands of people were treated with GH-3 at her Romanian clinic, including many leaders from around the world, such as Mao Tse-Tung, Charles de Gaulle, Ho Chi Minh, Winston Churchill, and John F. Kennedy. Even many Hollywood stars—including Dick Clark, the Gabor sisters, Marlene Dietrich, Charlie Chaplin, Lillian Gish, Lena Horne, Charles Bronson, Kirk Douglas, and Greta Garbo. All traveled to Romania for Dr. Aslan's GH-3 treatments.

Next generation formula is six times stronger than the GH-3 —and without the downside

While Dr. Aslan's results were extraordinary, her Procaine formula has its limitations—its beneficial effects wore off too quickly and the market was (and is) flooded by cheap and ineffective imitations. But now, through the HSI network, you and other members are among the very first in the United States to hear about H-3 Plus, the new and improved Procaine compound.

According to Gittleman, "H-3 Plus is the most advanced and only patented Procaine formula ever developed. It's so powerful, many people respond to it within the first three days. I have actually had to reduce my dosage to half a pill because it's so powerful."

The secret to the new formula lies in the purification process. H-3 Plus is run through a highly complex filtering process—making it 100 percent bioavailable. That means *all* the Procaine nutrients can be absorbed into the blood stream. Otherwise, Procaine leaves the body too quickly, providing only temporary relief.

H-3 Plus actually lasts 15 times longer and is 6 times stronger than Dr. Aslan's formula, which only delivered 15 percent of the nutrients and costs thousands of dollars to administer.

According to Gittleman, "H-3 Plus is a potent anti-aging supplement that keeps you feeling energized all day long. We have an enormous number of success stories from people who've felt relief from arthritis, depression, and lowered libido, and other chronic ailments associated with aging. We have even seen a return of some patients' original hair color. But most of all, you feel this overwhelming sense of well being." Gittleman added, "It's almost like an adaptogenic herb—it seems to provide whatever your body needs."

H-3 Plus is all-natural, and you don't have to go to Romania to get it

Like the original formula, H-3 Plus, now called Ultra H-3, is a completely natural substance, and you don't need a prescription. It comes in pill form and should be taken once or twice daily (six to eight hours apart) with a glass of water, one hour before or two hours after eating. For most people, taking Ultra H-3 twice a day on an empty stomach for three months gets the best results.

Ultra H-3 can be taken with other vitamins and supplements. In fact, your regular supplements may be absorbed more efficiently while taking it.

Through Health Sciences Institute's cutting-edge network of alternative doctors and researchers, members like you can be the first to benefit from this anti-aging breakthrough, and you don't have to travel to Romania to do so. If you want a powerful, all-natural way to slow, halt, and even reverse the aging process—you need to give Ultra H-3 a try. To find out what the "fountain of youth" can do for you refer to the Member Source Directory at the back of this report.

Chapter 3

Powerful antioxidant may save you from America's leading cause of blindness

On the shoreline of Kona, Hawaii, an industrial-sized incubator is cultivating microscopic algae. Normally such algae would be nothing more than fish food. But this algae may yield one of the world's most potent safeguards against cancer, heart disease, and blindness.

More than 13 million Americans over the age of 40 suffer from age-related macular degeneration (ARMD). This gradual decay of the macula—a cen-tral area of the retina that provides our most acute vision—is caused by ultraviolet light, air pollution, genetics, drug use, and countless other factors that degrade eye cells. ARMD produces irreversible vision loss and ranks as the single leading cause of blindness.

Researchers at Aquasearch Inc. of Hawaii and the University of Illinois Urbana-Champaign, however, believe they've discovered a phytonutrient in the ocean that could prevent the onset of ARMD...as well as lower the risk of cancer, cardiovascular disease, and neurodegenerative diseases.

At HSI, we've been looking for something that addresses ARMD for a long time. This is the first promising discovery we've found, and we thought you should know about it.

Study concludes nutrient is 80 times more effective than vitamin E

Astaxanthin [as-ta-zan-thin] is a xanthophyll (a derivative of the pigment, carotene). It's found in certain varieties of algae and produces a pink tint in the flesh of fish that consume it (namely, salmon, shrimp, crawfish, crab, lobster, and trout).

Laboratory research has demonstrated that astaxanthin has exceptional capabilities as an antioxidant (an agent that prevents the oxidation or mutation of cells) and an anti-inflammatory.[1,2] In recent animal studies at the College of Human Ecology in Seoul, Korea, astaxanthin protected the liver from toxin damage and stimulated the body's own cellular antioxidant system.[3]

Japanese researchers at the National Institute of Health and Nutrition conducted a placebo-controlled study on human subjects and found that astaxanthin inhibits the accumulation of LDL ("bad") cholesterol.[4]

Additional studies compared astaxanthin to other carotenoids and concluded that it's twice as effective as beta-carotene and nearly 80 times more effective than vitamin E at preventing oxidation within a chemical solution.[5]

Those results convinced some researchers that astaxanthin could quite capably deliver the same benefit as other antioxidants, namely lower the risk of cancer, heart diesease, high cholesterol, neurodegenerative diseases, and other age-related ailments. Now, researchers also surmise that it may help you keep your sight.

Carotenoids cross blood-brain barrier to protect eyes

To give your eyes extra protection, you may already be taking eye-specific antioxidants like lutein and zeaxanthin. Known collectively as xanthophylls, these carotenoids are found most abundantly in corn, kiwi, red seedless grapes, orange-colored peppers, spinach, celery, Brussel sprouts, scallions, broccoli, and squash.[6] And many people

include these foods or xanthophyll supplements in their diets to help prevent ARMD and cataracts. (Cataracts, which sometimes appear to be caused by light-induced oxidation of eye cells, currently afflict 14 percent of Americans over the age of 40.)

What makes xanthophylls special is their ability to affect the eyes. Not all antioxidants can do that, since not all are able to cross the blood-brain barrier (BBB). The BBB is a protective mechanism designed to prevent infectious organisms and chemicals from entering the nervous system. This is an effective way to prevent illness from spreading to areas that control life itself, such as the brain. Unfortunately, it also stops beneficial substances, like many antioxidants, from protecting those same organs. Very few antioxidants can penetrate the BBB. Lutein and zeaxanthin can. And so apparently can astaxanthin.

University of Illinois researchers Mark O.M. Tso, M.D., D.Sc., and Tim-Tak Lam, Ph.D., made this key discovery in tests on rats. In a successful petition to patent astaxanthin, they state, "The administration of astaxanthin also retards the progress of degenerative eye diseases and [benefits] the vision of the individuals suffering from degenerative eye diseases, such as age-related macular degeneration."[7]

Astaxanthin levels differ by 800 percent in wild and farmed fish

One simple way to benefit from astaxanthin is to include more fish containing this xanthophyll in your diet. Salmon is the richest source. However, not all salmon have the same chance to accumulate high levels of astaxanthin. Even though aquaculture operations supplement their fish food with astaxanthin, farmed salmon have dramatically less astaxanthin than do wild salmon. Different varieties of the fish raised in different stretches of ocean also contain different levels.

For example, farm-raised Atlantic salmon fed synthetic astaxanthin contain only 0.5 mg of the antioxidant in a 4-oz serving. Free-range sockeye salmon from the North Pacific that feed on wild microalgae containing natural astaxanthin, provide about 4.5 mg in a 4-oz serving.[8] By eating the right salmon variety, you could increase your astaxanthin intake by as much as 800 percent.

Patented incubator maximizes xanthophyll's production

A potent source of astaxanthin is a microalgae called *Haemotoccus pluvialis* (H. pluvialis) that grows in the rocky coastal areas around Hawaii. Scientists at Aquasearch Inc., a local biotechnology company, have harvested samples of H. pluvialis, studied them, and created special cultivating techniques to maximize the microalgae's production of astaxanthin.

After building high levels of the antioxidant in the microalgae, Aquasearch subjects the plant to a special churning process to break open the cells and release the astaxanthin. Next, the algae are pasteurized and dried at a low temperature, and the astaxanthin is extracted and sealed in a softgel capsule. Aquasearch markets the formula under the name AstaFactor. For ordering information, refer to the Member Source Directory at the back of this report.

Chapter 4

What your cells and space shuttles have in common— and how more of it can help your sex life

A few weeks ago, HSI panelist Allan Spreen, M.D., brought us news of a new, cutting-edge dietary supplement that he helped to develop as the Chief Research Advisor for NorthStar Nutritionals. This unique product, called Argi-Vive III, helps maintain sexual vitality and stamina in men from the most basic level. But the best part? Argi-Vive III is an effervescent, berry-flavored drink. So it's like drinking a glass of sparkling fruit juice that gives you the support you need without having to take another pill. It doesn't get much simpler than that.

The rocket science behind getting an erection

Argi-Vive III is a combination of niacin, vitamin B12, Panax ginseng root extract, catuaba bark, muira puama, ashwagandha root, gotu kola leaf, maca root, and horny goat weed. But the ingredient that packs the most punch is L-arginine. This amino acid plays a vital role as a precursor for nitric oxide (NO).

If you haven't heard of NO, it probably sounds a bit like rocket science, which isn't actually all that far off: Space shuttles do create this substance as they re-enter the atmosphere. So it's not too surprising that back in the 1970s, when professor Robert Furchgott first suggested that human cells also produce NO, he was met with quite a bit of skepticism.

But Furchgott's theory was confirmed when another group of researchers used a machine designed to detect NO in car exhaust fumes to test human cells. Sure enough, it was there. It turns out that the nitrogen in nitric oxide comes from the amino acid L-arginine and the oxygen comes from molecular oxygen.

As researchers learned more about how NO works in the human body, they found that your cells not only produce NO, but NO directly affects male sexual response. As far back as 1992, the National Institute of Health (NIH) acknowledged the effect NO has on male erectile function. Basically, it helps enhance circulation, which relaxes smooth muscles in the blood vessels, allowing them to become engorged with blood. And that results in an erection.

Activating your own NO cascade

Researchers at Hopkins discovered that the release of nitric oxide from nerve endings in the penis caused erections, but the temporary release of NO couldn't explain how erections are naturally sustained over time, since it survives just a few seconds before breaking down.

Working with rats and genetically transformed mice, Hopkins scientists found that after an initial burst of nitric oxide triggers an erection, blood vessels release more nitric oxide to harden and maintain it. As the lead researcher, Arthur Burnett, M.D., explained: "Once blood starts flowing into the penis, the source of nitric oxide in the blood vessels is continuously activated so that more nitric oxide is released, more tissue relaxes, more blood comes in, and a sustained erection is achieved."

Burnett says the cascade begins when erotic thoughts or physical sensations produce nitric oxide release in nerve endings in the penis. The flow of blood activates the release of more nitric oxide from the cells on the blood vessel walls (endothelial cells). The endothelial nitric oxide causes more tissue to relax, and the process repeats until the penis is fully erect.

In other words, the key element in getting and maintaining an erection is the continuous activation of nitric oxide. That's where L-arginine—and Argi-Vive III—come in. L-arginine is a precursor to NO. And Argi-Vive III contains 3,000 milligrams of it.

Argi-Vive III delivers L-arginine in a simple, unique, intelligent way—just mix one packet of powder with water, drink it like juice, and you're good to go for the day. L-arginine is water-soluble, so mixing the powder with water and drinking it enables it to work faster than tablets or capsules (which can take about 45 minutes to dissolve in your system).

A healthier sex life—and a healthier life overall

Two other nutrients in Argi-Vive III—vitamin B_{12} and niacin —support the star player L-arginine. Vitamin B_{12} is an essential nutrient that facilitates normal metabolism in cells and works in conjunction with folate to produce DNA and RNA. Animal trials have also shown that B_{12} can help maintain healthy male reproductive function, but more research needs to be done in humans. Niacin plays a vital role in providing chemical energy to the body.

But its benefits don't end there. Argi-Vive III also contains a proprietary blend of seven herbal extracts that have a long tradition of use for supporting sexual health, including catuaba bark, maca, and horny goat weed. The standout among the herbal ingredients, though, is Panax ginseng.

Recent studies on Panax ginseng show that it can increase NO synthesis in the endothelium of major organs, and it has also been shown to enhance the conversion of L-arginine to NO.

Convenient, great-tasting, risk-free support

NorthStar told me that they've already heard from a number of dedicated customers asking for more Argi-Vive III. Of course, it isn't just the L-arginine that's causing such a stir. Men are reporting that they love the convenience—and taste—of this new formula.

All in all, Argi-Vive III may be a great alternative to supporting sexual health and overall good health—without taking another pill. And using it is simple, since it comes in single-serving packets that you can take with you wherever you go. Just mix one packet with 8 ounces of water and drink once a day. For additional support, you can also try a second packet 30 to 60 minutes before sex.

And If you don't feel Argi-Vive III's powerful nutrients going to work for you, just let NorthStar Nutritionals know. They offer an exclusive 90-day unconditional guarantee for HSI Members only.

Chapter 5

HSI member's own kitchen concoction provides option to oral surgery

During a conversation with one of our members, Joe Lesky told me that back in 1997 his son Jim, 31 at the time, went for a regular dental checkup only to be told his gums were in such bad shape that his teeth either needed to be removed or they would fall out. This situation starts with gingivitis (inflammation of the gums), which is caused by plaque. If plaque isn't removed regularly, it grows and causes pockets between the teeth and gums. Healthy gums rest on the teeth without any gaps or pockets, but Jim's gums had pockets that measured 12 to 14 millimeters. Even half this measurement would have indicated a need for oral surgery. But Jim wasn't about to let the dentist pull any of his teeth. So

he went for a second opinion—same diagnosis.

Still not ready to give up his teeth, Jim went for a third opinion, this time to a periodontist who diagnosed him with severe gum infection and periodontal disease. What disturbed Jim most was that he had no idea that he even had gum disease. And he's not alone: According to the American Dental Association, three out of four adults over age 35 have some form of gum disease-and most people don't even realize it until the first signs of gum tenderness or some blood on their toothbrush. It seems that even with the current tooth-whitening trend, many of us have been neglecting our smiles. Or maybe the treatments that have been available to us so far are not living up to the need.

The periodontist treated him with an antibiotic for the infection, but, even after the infection was treated, he was told he still needed surgery to reduce the depth of gum pockets. Jim was still hesitant about having such a major procedure, so he called his dad for advice and help.

Joe Lesky had treated himself with homemade remedies for years and has compiled an extensive file of information on herbs and other natural healers. So when Jim called him asking for advice, Joe pulled out his herbal references, and, as he told me in our phone conversation, "After much research, I combined several herbal extracts and essential oils, which were reported to be beneficial to gum health."

The result was a powerful herbal mouthwash that combines:

- Cayenne—fights infection, stimulates circulation and healing, and relieves pain.
- Bloodroot—prevents bacteria from forming plaque via natural antiseptic properties.
- Echinacea—boosts the immune system, relieves pain, and acts as an antiseptic and antibacterial agent
- Bayberry—tightens and stimulates gums. Also an astringent
- White oak bark—eases inflammation, has astringent and antiseptic qualities, tightens gums
- Tea tree oil—offers protection from harmful bacteria and behaves as a natural antiseptic and anti-inflammatory.
- Peppermint oil—stimulates circulation and freshens breath.

Joe instructed his son to mix the formula with water and rinse with it every morning and night. Jim was skeptical, but he figured he had nothing to lose and might save his teeth.

A few weeks later, he went back to the periodontist for a checkup and cleaning. The periodontist noted that Jim's gums looked healthier and the pockets in them had gone down a little, but he would still need surgery. Jim bargained with the periodontist and got him to agree to wait several more months to see if he could achieve even better results using his father's homemade mouthwash.

A few months later, the pockets had gone down more and his gums were pink and healthy. The periodontist was pleased with the progress and they both agreed to hold off on the surgery indefinitely. Today

Jim's gums are still in good shape and he continues to use the solution regularly to keep them that way.

Even reverses oral bone loss

But even more amazing than Jim's return to gum health without surgery is that the bone loss associated with the severe infection had completely reversed. Many times, infections as severe as Jim's end up requiring bone grafts in order to replace lost bone. And that not only hurts your mouth-it also hurts your bank account. But Jim avoided this fate using the home made mouthwash, and he was able to reverse the deterioration altogether.

Sounds great, but we need more than one son's endorsement to cover a product in HSI. After all, this is just an herbal concoction that someone brewed up in his kitchen once, right? Well, as a matter of fact, Lesky wasn't just getting great results from his son—he was getting great results and feedback from a lot of his relatives, friends, and neighbors who had also tried his formula, and all wanted more. It seemed that the demand had outgrown his kitchen, so Lesky took the next step.

Coming to a store near you?

Lesky took the necessary steps of patenting his formula, designing and printing a label, and working with a manufacturer to produce 2,000 bottles of the product, which he named Peri-Gum. With that, the Lesky family hit the streets to get the word out locally. Joe, Jim, and Jim's wife Terri went around with cases to local health food stores telling of their successes with the formula. Joe even wrote an article for his local New Jersey paper.

Locally, Lesky received a phone call from a dentist detailing how a patient had brought in a copy of his article. It turned out that this dentist's wife and brother were both in need of oral surgery and were able to avoid it using Peri-Gum.

But getting the product out there on a national level didn't happen until a representative from a national natural product distributor heard about Peri-Gum. He also knew someone in need of oral surgery, and, once again, Peri-Gum offered that person effective healing without going under the knife. He was so impressed, he contacted Lesky and worked with him to bring Peri-Gum into health food stores nationwide.

Now Peri-Gum is available across the country. And it's even been the subject of several studies—all of which have confirmed that it works.

Most notably, one pilot study, completed at a prominent northeastern dental school, showed that volunteers' gum and oral health were significantly improved after just four weeks of using Peri-Gum. Researchers evaluated the subjects' progress by measuring the reduction of gingival health scores and reduction of plaque. Overall, they found a 20 percent reduction in the subjects' gingival health scores and a 16 percent reduction in plaque, And according to the study, Peri-Gum was found not to harm oral tissues.

Not what you'd expect from an ordinary mouthwash

The Peri-Gum concentrate formula is so powerful that when it's diluted with water according to the instructions, just one 1-oz. bottle makes up to 90 ounces of actual mouthwash. For use as a daily rinse, mix five drops of Peri-Gum with 1/2-oz. water and vigorously work the mouthwash between your teeth and gums for at least 30 seconds—the longer the better. Do not swallow.

Lesky recommends using Peri-Gum at least twice a day, especially at bedtime after you complete your normal dental hygiene routine (brushing teeth, etc.). He also suggests taking a very soft toothbrush, dipping it in the diluted Peri-Gum solution, and brushing with that instead of toothpaste.

I admit, my first reaction to a mouthwash containing cayenne was that it would burn—but I was game to at least try it. To my surprise, it didn't burn at all. But it did clean and refresh my mouth. In fact, it didn't just feel clean, it felt rejuvenated.

A leading developer and manufacturer of botanical extracts has picked up where Joe Lesky left off in his kitchen and has taken over the manufacturing of Peri-Gum, and now it's distributed across the country. You can purchase it in various health food stores or on-line directly through Lesky's company: Lesko Care, L.L.C. Contact information is listed in the Member Source Directory on page 126.

Chapter 6

An extract from the Oregon grape keeps skin smooth and supple

Problem skin is not only uncomfortable and frustrating, it can also be embarrassing for many. And for some, it can actually be aggravated by stress. From your scalp, knees, elbows, and ears...to all over. Conventional remedies offering only temporary relief options leave much to be desired.

Mahonia aquifolium: For those serious about skin health

A product made from an extract of mahonia aquifolium (also known as the Oregon grape) is showing great signs of success with thousands of sufferers. In 1995, researchers in 89 dermatology practices throughout Germany put mahonia aquifolium to the test, using 433 patients who suffered from chronic psoriasis. Over the course of 12 weeks, the dermatologists reported that symptoms improved or completely disappeared in 81 percent of the patients.[1]

60 years of suffering overcome within a month

For 60 years, Peggy Sterling tried everything she could find to relieve the ugly, itchy patches of angry red that covered nearly her entire body—without success.

Then Peggy tried mahonia aquifolium. Within a month, she felt relief. For the first time since her teens, her skin was clear and smooth. "Quite literally, within days my skin was improved," Peggy reported.

Extracts available for daytime and nighttime use

There are a number of products based on mahonia aquifolium, marketed under the brand name of M-Folia. Most useful for psoriasis suffers are the cream and ointment preparations. Both contain the same strength of mahonia aquifolium (10 percent extract). Many find the ideal solution is to use the cream during the day and the ointment at night (since the ointment can rub off on clothing and make the skin appear greasy).

Safe, non-toxic, and effective

M-Folia products are extremely safe and appropriate for use even on small children. Although M-Folia can be used in combination with other treatments, please double-check with your doctor if you are using any other medications or if you are pregnant. A few people experience a temporary initial worsening of symptoms, which soon passes. Refer to the back of this report for ordering information.

Chapter 7

Herbal-tea extract lowers blood sugar and helps patients lose weight —without changes in diet or exercise

Diabetes afflicts over 16 million Americans. The American diet—processed foods high in sugar, low in fiber, and virtually devoid of nutrients—combined with a sedentary lifestyle, has caused the disease to spread rapidly. But Type II diabetes (noninsulin dependent) doesn't happen overnight. It usually takes five to 10 years before a recurring set of circumstances repeats itself enough times and causes enough damage to result in diabetes.

Gerald M. Reaven, M.D., of Stanford University Medical Center, coined the term "Syndrome X" to describe the blood sugar disorder that leads to Type II diabetes. If you have Syndrome X, you're insulin resistant—a dangerous situation since insulin processes the sugar in your blood and converts it to glycogen, which is stored in your liver and muscles for later use.

In the case of insulin resistance, your cells don't respond quickly enough to insulin production and you have high blood sugar levels for longer periods of time. Your body senses that there's too much blood sugar and produces even more insulin.

Instead of being processed by the extra insulin, your body responds negatively and keeps your blood sugar levels high. This is a self-perpetuating cycle that leads to increased resistance to insulin and even higher levels of blood sugar. As a result, your cells don't get the energy they need—leaving you tired and groggy. Your body responds to this condition by craving more sugar for fuel. So you eat again, flooding your system with even more glucose, and heading down the road to Type II diabetes.

Although Type II diabetics usually produce insulin, their bodies are unable to process insulin efficiently and would benefit from a supplement to help transport glucose out of the blood and convert it to glycogen for storage. In some cases, Type II diabetics don't produce sufficient amounts of insulin and may require oral medication or insulin injections.

If you have Syndrome X, it's very likely that you also have elevated triglyceride levels, low HDL ("good" cholesterol), high LDL or VLDL ("bad" cholesterol), high blood pressure, and the slow clearing of fat from the blood.

Factors that increase your risk of contracting Syndrome X include stress, obesity, lack of physical activity, high-carbohydrate intake, a low-fiber diet, excessive alcohol consumption, polycystic ovaries, and smoking. If you're in the high-risk group for Syndrome X and don't do anything to improve your situation, you'll most likely end up with Type II diabetes. While many of the risk factors can be addressed through changes in your lifestyle, reducing blood sugar levels hasn't been very easy if you're insulin resistant. Until now.

Banaba plant lowers blood sugar by 32 percent—in just three weeks

The banaba is a medicinal plant commonly found in the Philippines and Southeast Asia. Its leaves were traditionally brewed to make a tea used to counteract diabetes and high blood sugar. Researchers found that corosolic acid was the active ingredient in the leaves, so they standardized the extract and created a product called Glucosol.™

William V. Judy, Ph.D., of the Southeastern Institute of Biomedical Research in Bradenton, Florida, used Glucosol in animal and human clinical trials to determine if its effects could help mild-to-moderate Type II diabetics reduce their blood-sugar levels. Last year, Dr. Judy conducted five human clinical trials (unpublished) that attempted to reduce diabetics' elevated fasting glucose levels, which averaged 150 milligrams/deciliter (normal levels are 70 to 110 milligrams/ deciliter).

In the first study, 22 Type II diabetics were given 16, 32, or 48 milligrams of Glucosol per day. The resulting decrease in diabetic symptoms was nothing short of astounding. Patients receiving 48 milligrams per day had the most pronounced decrease in their blood sugar levels. After just 20 days, they reduced those levels by an average of 32 percent and lost an average of two pounds without making any changes in their diet or exercise regimen. Three other studies using 48 milligrams of Glucosol per day duplicated those significant blood sugar reductions. The herb appears to work by improving the rate at which sugar is transported out of your blood but doesn't reduce your blood sugar excessively.

Glucosol helps you lose weight without disrupting normal blood sugar levels

To determine if weight loss could be experienced by nondiabetics who take the herbal extract, Glucosol was given to 10 test subjects who did not have a history of blood sugar disorders. The patients were supplemented with 48 mg of Glucosol every day for 30 days. By the end of the test period, the average weight loss experienced by the normal subjects was 2.4 pounds. Two weeks after the end of the test period, the patients had not only maintained their

weight loss, they had lost even more weight! Their average weight loss increased slightly to 2.6 pounds. None of the subjects experienced any difficulty with hypoglycemia (low blood sugar), which indicates that Glucosol doesn't transport more sugar out of your blood than is required.

With Glucosol, diabetes doesn't have to be the road to serious health problems

Glucosol and insulin supplements work in different ways. The risks you experience with insulin supplements—either too-low or too-high blood sugar levels—don't happen with Glucosol. Available without a prescription, this herbal extract can help you get control of your blood sugar levels and avoid the serious consequences of diabetes.

Glucosol is available as Sugarsolve.™ For ordering information, see the Member Source Directory on page 126.

Chapter 8

Believe it when you see it:
3-nutrient eyedrop formula dissolves cataracts without surgery

If you're like me, you don't like putting anything in your eye. Even thinking about it makes me nervous. And the thought of eye surgery? Forget it. But develop cataracts, and it's either surgery or blindness, right? Not anymore.

Doctors in Europe have developed eyedrops with a natural ingredient that can safely and painlessly break up cataracts. These drops have been used successfully in Britain since they were introduced there several years ago, and now they're also available in the U.S.

TV show trial sparks interest in natural cataract solution

OcuPhase combines N-acetyl L-carnosine (a.k.a. NAC) with vitamins A and E and appears to have the ability to reverse the aging process of cells that lead to cataracts.

The formula was originally introduced in Europe by Professor Steven Charles Gallant, after his father's experience with cataracts led him to investigate NAC more closely. Gallant had been studying another carnosine derivative, L-carnosine, for many years. When his father developed cataracts and was reluctant to go under the knife,

Gallant remembered that the NAC form of carnosine had been proven in previous studies to have positive effects on the condition.

"I tried to get some for him," Gallant explained, "but unfortunately, at the time, it wasn't easily obtainable. My father had to have the operation, which thankfully was successful. But that got me to thinking how great it would be if we were to develop, and make readily available, a product that could address this condition with a simple course of eye drops as opposed to invasive surgery."

After many years of research and development, Gallant came up with an eyedrop formula he called Bright Eyes, which is the basis for the OcuPhase formula available here in the U.S.

In Europe, it seems to have gained popularity after being featured on a U.K. television program called *The Richard & Judy TV Trials* show.[1]

The show conducted its own short experimental trial to see if the eye drops could live up to their claim of improving vision. The four people who tried it (including the hostess, Judy) did say they noticed their vision had improved.

After seeing the show, hundreds of other people tried the Bright Eyes formula. I'll fill you in on some of those testimonials in a minute, but right now let's talk a bit about the mechanics behind cataracts and what's wrong with conventional treatments for it.

Why you're not seeing clearly

The lens of the eye is made up mostly of protein and water that combine as a clear tissue that allows light to pass through and focus on the retina. Over time, the tissue can become damaged by free radicals that occur as a result of any number of reasons—diabetes, long-term use of corticosteriods, heredity, ultra- violet light, poor nutrition, smoking, high blood pressure, aging, etc.

One of the other major causes of damage to the eye is glycation. Glycation occurs when sugars combine with proteins to create a whole new type of compound called glycated proteins, which produce 50 times more free radicals than normal proteins. The end result is that the water-soluble structural proteins in the lens of the eye clump together, or become cross-linked. (They also become oversaturated with water, creating internal pressure in the eye.) This causes the characteristic clouding of the eye lens associated with cataracts. Think of it like cooking an egg white: It's clear and fluid as it hits the pan, but as it becomes stressed by the heat, it becomes opaque and rubbery.

The fix? We need to break down these protein cross-links, restore transparency, and reduce internal pressure—and that's precisely what OcuPhase eyedrops do. But before we talk about how OcuPhase clears the eye lens, let's talk about the most common treatment option for cataracts.

Surgery isn't always a one-time solution

During cataract surgery, the damaged lens is removed and replaced with a synthetic lens implant. Sounds simple, but it turns out that cataract surgery is a two-part ordeal.

The new lens implant is held in place inside the eye by a thin membrane called the posterior capsule, part of the original covering of the lens that is intentionally left behind for this purpose. The problem is, in up to 50 percent of patients who have this procedure, the lens capsule begins clouding up again within two years. This isn't quite the same thing as the cataract coming back, since the cloudy

posterior capsule is much thinner than the original cataract, and it can be opened up with a laser beam.

The corrective procedure is considered a "follow-up visit" and can apparently be done in the opthalmologist's office. But to those of us who are squeamish about this sort of thing to begin with, having to do it twice is hardly a selling point—especially considering the other possible complications, like glaucoma, detached retinas, corneal edema, severely compromised corneas requiring corneal transplants, and internal eye infections, which can all potentially cause complete loss of vision.

Apparently, I'm not the only one who finds this option less than appealing. Our contacts at Pure Tango, Inc. also saw a need for more options, which is why they worked to develop OcuPhase: their own version of the highly effective and successful British Bright Eyes formula.

Nutrient drops work from the outside in

The Pure Tango OcuPhase formula contains NAC, vitamin A, and vitamin E. Vitamin A is essential for the health and function of epithelial cells, the cells in the top-most layer of tissues like those in the lens of the eye. When it's used topically in the eye, vitamin E can increase the survival time of corneal endothelial cells, decrease inflammation, speed up healing of eye tissues, regenerate gluta-thione in the eye (which naturally decreases with age), and even prevent cataracts in some animal studies.[2-7] Add the power of NAC, which seems to act synergistically with vitamin E, and the vitamin combination is suddenly supercharged.[8] But what exactly makes NAC so effective?

The NAC in OcuPhase acts as a time-release version of L-carnosine. It's important to understand that OcuPhase isn't "just" L-carnosine in eyedrop form. Apparently, the results from NAC are achieved safely because of its time-release action: It breaks down and transforms into L-carnosine gradually. To speed up the process could ultimately cause more damage to the eye.

What's amazing is that even though our eyes and lenses are very impermeable, NAC is able to slowly permeate the lens structure. It's able to do this because unlike straight carnosine, NAC is soluble in lipids as well as in water.[9] The eyes contain both.

So after it enters the lipid components of the eye,

NAC transforms into L-carnosine. This small molecule performs a remarkable variety of functions—most notably anti-oxidation and anti-glycation.

L-carnosine actually restores the lens by removing those cross-linked protein groups we talked about earlier. A 1999 Chinese study demonstrated that carnosine has a 100 percent success rate on early-stage senile cataracts and an 80 percent success rate on more advanced cases.[10]

Vision improves in 90 percent of study participants

I found that most of the recent research on N-acetyl carnosine has been carried out in Russia—all with encouraging results.[11-13]

In a 2001 study, Russian scientists conducted two randomized, double-blind, placebo-controlled trials—one for six months, one for 24 months—using an NAC eyedrop formula. A total of 49 patients (average age 65) with cataracts ranging in severity from minimal to advanced (but not to the point of requiring surgery) were treated with two drops of the NAC solution per day. The team monitored the condition of the cataracts, visual acuity, and glare sensitivity.

They found that the eyes treated with NAC were substantially improved in six months— transmissivity (the amount of light penetrating the lens of the eye) increased in 42 percent; glare sensitivity improved in 89 percent; and overall vision improved in 90 percent of the study participants. Even more good news: These improvements held up for the entire 24-month duration of the trial. And there was no worsening in any of the NAC-treated eyes, whereas visual acuity dropped in 89 percent of the controls after 24 months.[14]

British customers back up eyedrops' benefits

As I mentioned earlier, the OcuPhase formula has just become available in the U.S., so there isn't much feedback on it yet. But the very similar Bright Eyes formula has been available in Britain for some time. The following letters were written to the British distributor of Bright Eyes after it was featured in several articles and on the *Richard & Judy* TV show.

"I want to tell you about my experiences with the special eye-drops. At first I didn't think there were any real differences, but I persisted in using the drops twice a day in the affected eye. Now after about three months I believe that there are significant changes to my vision. It's been a fairly gradual thing, which may explain why I didn't appreciate any changes early on, but now it's obvious to me that my eyesight has improved. The changes are slower than I anticipated, but I for one am sold on the drops!"

—C.B.S.

"Some 10 years ago I was told I was developing cataracts from the outside of my eyes to the inside. Five years ago I was told I must not drive: having never learnt I was not too upset. But two years ago I was warned that the cataracts were just about fully formed and I needed check-ups every six months… I have now been using carnosine eye drops for six months. I recently went to the optician and was told I only had a bit of a cataract. Also I do not need to see an optician for two years. I could not believe it… So very, very many thanks. My husband went to the optician last week, and he is just starting to form a cataract in his right eye. Needless to say he will be using carnosine eye drops."

—J.C.

"In October 2002, I was diagnosed with a small cataract in my left eye. Shortly afterwards a work colleague told me about the eye drops as seen on channel 4 'Richard & Judy.' I started using them. In April 2004, I had an in-depth eye test: NO SIGN OF THE CATARACT."

—M.S.

See for yourself

As a preventive, the suggested use of OcuPhase is one or two drops in each eye every day. Those with any kind of eye problem may want to apply one or two drops several times a day. Most people report that they start noticing positive results over a three to six month period. Early intervention allows OcuPhase to work even better, since the lens is more permeable in the early stages.

Keep in mind that even though this treatment can be done in the comfort of your own home, it's always a good idea to work with your healthcare provider to assure safety and to monitor your progress.

Member Source Directory

Argi-Vive III, NorthStar Nutritionals. (888)856-1489; www.northstarnutritionals.com. A month supply (30 packets) is US $49.95 plus shipping.

Astafactor, Mera Pharmaceuticals, Inc. 73-4460 Queen Kaahumanu Hwy., Suite 110, Kailuakona, HI 96740; tel: (800)480-6515 or (808)326-9301; fax: (808)326-9401; www.astafactor.com

M-Folia, NorthStar Nutritionals, P.O. Box 970, Frederick, MD 21705; (888)856-1489; www.northstarnutritionals.com

Sugarsolve, Harmony Company, P.O. Box 93, Northvale, NJ 07447; tel:(888)809-1241; www.theharmonyco.com.

OcuPhase Eyedrops, Smart Nutrition; ph. (800)599-8607. A box of 2 x 5 ml vials costs US$41.95, approximately a one month supply. HSI Members purchasing 3 or more boxes of OcuPhase will receive free shipping to anywhere in the U.S.

Oralmat, GoldShield Healthcare Direct, 1501 Northpoint Parkway, Suite 100, West Palm beach, FL 33407; tel. (800)474-9495; www.goldshieldusa.com

Peri-Gum, Lesko Care, L.L.C; tel: (908)272-3081; www.peri-gum.com. A 1-oz. bottle of concentrate is US$17.95 plus US$4.95 shipping and handling. Online orders only, using PayPal. Website also offers individual state listings of retailers carrying Peri-Gum or by mail at Lesko Care, LLC 18 Connecticut Street, Cranford, NJ 07016.

Ultra H-3, Uni Key Health Systems, Inc., 181 West Commerce Drive, Hayden Lake, ID 83835; tel: (800)888-4353; www.unikeyhealth.com

Please note: HSI receives no compensation for providing editorial coverage for the products that appear in your Members Alert. HSI is a subsidiary of the same holding company as NDI Solutions, the distributor of NorthStar Nutritionals, RealAdvantage and Pure Country Naturals supplements.

References

Australian breakthrough against asthma and allergies

[1] Reynolds, "Editorial for the Australian Naturopathic Practioners and Chircopractors Association Practitioner Journal" March 1996

Turn back the clock with nature's new fountain of youth

[1] *Science* 2000;287: 2486-92

[2] www.smart-drugs.com/ias-info/gh3-prevention.htm

Powerful antioxidant may save you from America's leading cause of blindness

[1] *Lipids* 1989;24(7): 659-61

[2] *Physiological Chemistry and Physics and Medical NMR* 1990;22(1): 27-38

[3] *Methods and Findings in Experimental and Clinical Pharmacology* 2001;23(2): 79-84

[4] *Journal of Atherosclerosis and Thrombosis* 2000;7(4): 216-22

[5] www.astaxanthin.org

[6] *The British Journal of Ophthalmology* 1998;82(8): 907-10

[7] United States Patent No. 5,527,533;Tso, Mark O.M. and Lam, Tim-Tak; October 27, 1994

[8] *Journal of AOAC International* 1997;80(3): 622-32

An extract from the Oregon grape keeps skin smooth and supple

[1] *Journal of Dermatological Treatment* 1995;6: 31-34

[2] *Planta Medica* 1995;61: 372-73

Believe it when you see it: 3-nutrient eyedrop formula dissolves cataracts without surgery

[1] http://www.ethos.ag/video/randj-update-1.wmv (video clip of Richard & Judy TV Trials Show)

[2] *Ophthalmologica* 2001; 215(3): 192-6

[3] *Aust N Z J Ophthalmol* 1987;15(4): 309-14

[4] *J Ocul Pharmacol Ther* 1999; 15(4): 345-350

[5] *Exp Eye Res* 1999; 68(6): 747-755

[6] *Ann Nutr Metab* 1999; 43(5): 286-289

[7] *Klin Oczna* 1998; 100(2): 85-88

[8] *Age and Ageing* 2000; 29: 207-210

[9] *Photochemistry and Photobiology* 2000; 71(5): 559-566

[10] Wang AM, et al. "Use of carnosine as a natural anti-senescence drug for human beings." Department of Biochemistry and Department of Neurobiology, Harbin Medical University, China, 1999

[11] Babizhayev MA, Deyev A. "Free radical oxidation of lipid and thiol groups in genesis of cataract." *Biophysics* (biofizika) 1986; 31: 119-125

[12] Babizhayev MA, Deyev Al, Linberg LF. "Lipid peroxidation as a possible cause of cataract." *Mech Ageing Dev* 1988; 44: 69-89

[13] Babizhayev MA. "Antioxidant activity of L-carnosine, a natural histidine-containing di-peptide in crystalline lens." *Biochem Biophys Acta* 1989; 1,004: 363-371

[14] Babizhayev MA, Deyev AI, Yermakova VN, et al. "N-Acetylcarnosine, a natural histidine-containing dipeptide, as a potent ophthalmic drug in treatment of human cataracts." *Peptides* 2001; 22: 979-994